Growing in the Gospel

The Psalms Project Volume Two

Discovering the Spiritual World through the Psalms – Psalm 11 to 20

Michael Harvey Koplitz

TABLE OF CONTENTS

Michael Harvey Koplitz

The Goal of this project:

This research project will examine the 150 psalms for the spiritual awareness each Psalm offers. Each Psalm will be examined by its language and the commentary of the Sages. The spiritual awareness analysis will be done in alignment with Ari's definition of the Tree of life, the Book of Creation, and the Zohar. Each verse of the Psalm will be rewritten using the intent of the language and spiritual commentary to convey its spiritual lesson.

The Main Resources:

The Zohar

The Book of Creation

Ari's writing on the Tree of Life and the Ten Sefirot

The Theological Wordbook of the Old Testament

Samson Hirsch's commentary on the Psalms

Tehillim – Psalms – A new translation with a commentary anthologized from the Talmudic and rabbinic sources

Accordance Bible Software

Michael Harvey Koplitz

Psalm Eleven

New American Standard 1995	Hebrew

Psa. 11:0 For the choir director. *A Psalm* of David.
¹ In the LORD I take refuge;
    How can you say to my soul,
"Flee *as* a bird to your mountain;
²   For, behold, the wicked bend the bow,
    They make ready their arrow upon the string
    To shoot in darkness at the upright in heart.
³   If the foundations are destroyed,
    What can the righteous do?"
 	
Psa. 11:4   The LORD is in His holy temple; the LORD'S throne is in Heaven;
    His eyes behold, His eyelids test the sons of men.
⁵   The LORD tests the righteous and the wicked,
    And the one who loves violence His soul hates.
⁶   Upon the wicked He will rain snares;
    Fire and brimstone and burning wind will be the portion of their cup.
⁷   For the LORD is righteous, He loves righteousness;
    The upright will behold His face.
	Psa. 11:1 לַמְנַצֵּחַ לְדָוִד בַּיהוָה ׀
	חָסִיתִי אֵיךְ תֹּאמְרוּ לְנַפְשִׁי
	נוּדִי [נוּדוּ] הַרְכֶם צִפּוֹר ׃ ² כִּי
	הִנֵּה הָרְשָׁעִים יִדְרְכוּן קֶשֶׁת
	כּוֹנְנוּ חִצָּם עַל־יֶתֶר לִירוֹת
	בְּמוֹ־אֹפֶל לְיִשְׁרֵי־לֵב ׃ ³ כִּי
	הַשָּׁתוֹת יֵהָרֵסוּן צַדִּיק מַה־
	פָּעָל ׃ ⁴ יְהוָה ׀ בְּהֵיכַל קָדְשׁוֹ
	יְהוָה בַּשָּׁמַיִם כִּסְאוֹ עֵינָיו יֶחֱזוּ
	עַפְעַפָּיו יִבְחֲנוּ בְּנֵי אָדָם ׃ ⁵
	יְהוָה צַדִּיק יִבְחָן וְרָשָׁע וְאֹהֵב
	חָמָס שָׂנְאָה נַפְשׁוֹ ׃ ⁶ יַמְטֵר עַל־
	רְשָׁעִים פַּחִים אֵשׁ וְגָפְרִית וְרוּחַ
	זִלְעָפוֹת מְנָת כּוֹסָם ׃ ⁷ כִּי־
	צַדִּיק יְהוָה צְדָקוֹת אָהֵב יָשָׁר
	יֶחֱזוּ פָנֵימוֹ ׃

Targum

Psa. 11:1 A hymn of David. In the word of the LORD I have hoped; how do you say to my soul, wander to the mountain like a bird? [2] For behold, the wicked bend the bow, fixing their arrows on the string to shoot in darkness at the firm of heart. [3] For if the foundations are shattered, why did the virtuous do good? [4] The LORD is in his temple; God's throne is in the highest heavens; his eyes see, his eyelids examine, the sons of men. [5] God examines the righteous, but his soul hates the wicked and those who love rapacity. [6] He will bring down rains of retribution on the wicked, coals of fire and brimstone; a violent storm-wind is the portion of their cup. [7] For the LORD is righteous, he loves righteousness, the honest man will look upon his countenance.

Verse One

New American Standard 1995	Hebrew
Psa. 11:0 For the choir director. *A Psalm* of David. ¹ In the LORD I take refuge; How can you say to my soul, "Flee *as* a bird to your mountain;	לַמְנַצֵּחַ לְדָוִד בַּיהוָה ׀ חָסִיתִי אֵיךְ תֹּאמְרוּ לְנַפְשִׁי נוּדוּ [נֹוּדִי] הַרְכֶם צִפּוֹר

Verse Analysis

This Psalm is a sequel to Psalm 10 because it tries to answer why wicked people prosper while the righteous suffer.

A mountain is a symbol of stability. The bird denotes something unstable and easily moveable. The Sage Rashi said that David wrote this Psalm when he was fleeing from Saul's men. They were trying to capture David to kill him. So David hid in the caves in the mountains to elude the men.

נוּדוּ (nudu) is in the plural form. The verb means "to flee." Why did David use the plural form of the verb? The Sage Radak said that the men wanting to kill David wanted his body and his soul destroyed. If David's soul was destroyed, then he could not find rest in Heaven. His existence would have been wiped out on Earth and in Heaven.

"Flee for your mountain is a bird" is an interesting phrase. The mountain symbolizes stability, and for David, that stability was His faith and trust in the LORD. Why would the LORD tell Him that his faith was like a bird, which means that it was unstable? To fully grasp this, the concept of where the LORD's influence on Earth in David's day must be examined. The people of David's day believed that the LORD's influence was only in Eretz Israel (the land of Israel). Therefore, David was surprised that the LORD was telling him to leave Eretz Israel. David was confused that the LORD would tell him to leave His presence. However, the LORD knew that if David stayed inside the borders of Eretz Israel that Saul's men would capture and kill him. Therefore, the verse is saying that the security of the LORD was not secure for David. Saul's men were going to find him and kill him.

Verse Rewrite Emphasizing Spiritual Awareness

For the conductor, a psalm of David. In the LORD, I took refuge from my evil enemies. Why, LORD, would you tell me to leave Eretz Israel and your protection?

Verse Two

New American Standard 1995	Hebrew

2   For, behold, the wicked bend the bow,
    They make ready their arrow upon the string
    To shoot in darkness at the upright in heart.
	כִּי הִנֵּה הָרְשָׁעִים יִדְרְכוּן 2
	
	קֶשֶׁת כּוֹנְנוּ חִצָּם עַל־יֶתֶר
	
	לִירוֹת בְּמוֹ־אֹפֶל לְיִשְׁרֵי־לֵב׃

Verse Analysis

Wicked people are quick and ready to kill the righteous. They will shoot an arrow to kill the righteous even if they cannot see them. They hate everything proper and good in the world.

Verse Rewrite Emphasizing Spiritual Awareness

Wicked people are always ready to kill a righteous person.

Verse Three

New American Standard 1995	Hebrew
3 If the foundations are destroyed, What can the righteous do?"	כִּי הַשָּׁתוֹת יֵהָרֵסוּן צַדִּיק מַה־3 פָּעָל :

Verse Analysis

What are the foundations? The LORD's moral and ethical order is the foundation of the Universe. However, what happens if the foundation becomes rotten? This situation allows evil and wickedness to triumph. There is nothing to stop them. The pillars of justice and law will stop evil, but not when they are either removed from society or the enforces of justice and law decide not to enforce them anymore.

Verse Rewrite Emphasizing Spiritual Awareness

When justice and law are removed from your creation LORD, what can a righteous man do to restore them?

Verse Four

New American Standard 1995	Hebrew
Psa. 11:4 The LORD is in His holy temple; the LORD'S throne is in Heaven; His eyes behold, His eyelids test the sons of men.	4 יְהוָה ׀ בְּהֵיכַל קָדְשׁוֹ יְהוָה בַּשָּׁמַיִם כִּסְאוֹ עֵינָיו יֶחֱזוּ עַפְעַפָּיו יִבְחֲנוּ בְּנֵי אָדָם׃

Verse Analysis

כְּסֵה (keeseh) – means "throne." It also denotes that the LORD's throne is more than just a throne in the Heavens. The entire Universe is a part of the LORD's throne. Since the LORD retracted to create the Universe (from the Book of Creation), the Universe is always a part of the LORD. Therefore, the LORD's throne encompasses everything.

The LORD sees everything, the all-seeing eye. The eyelids remind humans that they can do things that do not get recognized immediately by the LORD, thus closing the eyelids. However, the eyelids do open, and the LORD will see everything. Therefore, it is a fallacy to think that the LORD's eyelids close at any time. They are always open and always watching what is happening in His creation.

Verse Rewrite Emphasizing Spiritual Awareness

The LORD resides on His throne in Heaven and sees everything all the time.

Verse Five

New American Standard 1995	Hebrew
5 The LORD tests the righteous and the wicked, And the one who loves violence His soul hates.	יְהֹוָה צַדִּיק יִבְחָן וְרָשָׁע וְאֹהֵב חָמָס שָׂנְאָה נַפְשׁוֹ׃

Verse Analysis

It always appears odd that the LORD test the righteous. Testing the wicked makes sense because the LORD wants to see if the wicked person turns away from their wicked ways. Why constantly test the righteous? The Sages tell us that the more righteous one is, the more intense the testing from the LORD. For example, Abraham proved his love for the LORD when he destroyed his father's idols. He showed the LORD his love on many other occasions. However, the LORD tested Abraham no less than ten times. The thought is that the righteous are tested to increase their righteousness. The LORD prepares the righteous for the world to come (Heaven). Each test to a righteous person is a lesson that the LORD wants them to learn before He will allow the person to enter Heaven. The LORD dispenses with wicked people because it is known that the wicked person will not change. Therefore, why would the LORD want to deal with such a person?

Verse Rewrite Emphasizing Spiritual Awareness

The LORD constantly is testing the righteous and the wicked. The wicked person who decides to remain wicked the LORD will not allow in Heaven.

Verse Six

New American Standard 1995	Hebrew
6 Upon the wicked He will rain snares; Fire and brimstone and burning wind will be the portion of their cup.	יַמְטֵר עַל־רְשָׁעִים פַּחִים אֵשׁ וְגָפְרִית וְרוּחַ זִלְעָפוֹת מְנָת כּוֹסָם׃

Verse Analysis

יַמְטֵר (yametare) - this word means "rain." However, it denotes more than just rain. It denotes anything that comes from the LORD's Heaven.

פַּחִים (pacheem) – this word means "traps." David was referring to the victims of unsuspecting traps that catch the feet. There are many traps that the LORD can send, but also there are traps that society develops. For example, prosperity can turn a person's heart away from charity. The desire to have as many valuables as possible can pollute the mind. Then, the person forgets about the poor people.

The LORD sends fire, brimstone, and wind to wicked people. An example is what the LORD sent to Sodom and Gemorrah. When Lot and his family evacuated the city, the LORD sent fire, brimstone and wind to destroy the wicked city.

Verse Rewrite Emphasizing Spiritual Awareness

He sends traps for wicked people; fire, brimstone, and wind are sent to the lover of violence whom the LORD despises.

Verse Seven

New American Standard 1995	Hebrew
7 For the LORD is righteous, He loves righteousness; The upright will behold His face.	כִּי־צַדִּיק יְהוָה צְדָקוֹת אָהֵב 7 יָשָׁר יֶחֱזוּ פָנֵימוֹ׃

Verse Analysis

There are many times throughout history that the LORD's way does not make any sense to humans. For example, David did not understand why the LORD told him to leave Eretz Israel. David did not understand that the LORD is the LORD of all creation, which means that no matter where David went on the Earth, the LORD was with him. So, to David, the LORD's command to leave Eretz Israel seemed crazy. However, David did obey the LORD and understood that it is unnecessary to comprehend what the LORD wants a person to do.

Verse Rewrite Emphasizing Spiritual Awareness

For the LORD is righteous, He loves righteous people; He will show His love to the righteous.

Complete Psalm Rewrite Emphasizing Spiritual Awareness

For the conductor, a psalm of David. In the LORD, I took refuge from my evil enemies. Why, LORD, would you tell me to leave Eretz Israel and your protection?

Wicked people are always ready to kill a righteous person.

When justice and law are removed from your creation LORD, what can a righteous man do to restore them.

The LORD resides on His throne in Heaven and sees everything all the time.

The LORD constantly is testing the righteous and the wicked. The wicked person who decides to remain wicked the LORD will not allow in Heaven.

He sends traps for wicked people; fire, brimstone, and wind are sent to the lover of violence whom the LORD despises.

For the LORD is righteous, He loves righteous people; He will show His love to the righteous.

Michael Harvey Koplitz

Psalm Twelve

New American Standard 1995	Hebrew
For the choir director; upon an eight-stringed lyre. A Psalm of David	Psa. 12:1 לַמְנַצֵּחַ עַל־הַשְּׁמִינִית
Psa. 12:1 Help, LORD, for the godly man ceases to be,	מִזְמוֹר לְדָוִד ׃ 2 הוֹשִׁיעָה יְהוָה כִּי־ גָמַר חָסִיד כִּי־פַסּוּ אֱמוּנִים מִבְּנֵי
For the faithful disappear from among the sons of men.	אָדָם ׃ 3 שָׁוְא יְדַבְּרוּ אִישׁ אֶת־
2 They speak falsehood to one another;	רֵעֵהוּ שְׂפַת חֲלָקוֹת בְּלֵב וָלֵב
With flattering lips and with a double heart they speak.	יְדַבֵּרוּ ׃ 4 יַכְרֵת יְהוָה כָּל־שִׂפְתֵי
3 May the LORD cut off all flattering lips,	חֲלָקוֹת לָשׁוֹן מְדַבֶּרֶת גְּדֹלוֹת ׃ 5
The tongue that speaks great things;	אֲשֶׁר אָמְרוּ ׀ לִלְשֹׁנֵנוּ נַגְבִּיר
4 Who have said, "With our tongue we will prevail;	שְׂפָתֵינוּ אִתָּנוּ מִי אָדוֹן לָנוּ ׃ 6 מִשֹּׁד
Our lips are our own; who is lord over us?"	עֲנִיִּים מֵאַנְקַת אֶבְיוֹנִים עַתָּה אָקוּם
5 "Because of the devastation of the afflicted, because of the groaning of the needy,	יֹאמַר יְהוָה אָשִׁית בְּיֵשַׁע יָפִיחַ לוֹ ׃
Now I will arise," says the LORD; "I will ʿset him in the safety for which he longs."	7 אִמְרוֹת יְהוָה אֲמָרוֹת טְהֹרוֹת כֶּסֶף צָרוּף בַּעֲלִיל לָאָרֶץ מְזֻקָּק
Psa. 12:6 The words of the LORD are pure words;	שִׁבְעָתָיִם ׃ 8 אַתָּה־יְהוָה תִּשְׁמְרֵם תִּצְּרֶנּוּ ׀ מִן־הַדּוֹר זוּ לְעוֹלָם ׃ 9
As silver tried in a furnace on the earth, refined seven times.	סָבִיב רְשָׁעִים יִתְהַלָּכוּן כְּרֻם זֻלּוּת
7 You, O LORD, will keep them;	לִבְנֵי אָדָם ׃
You will preserve him from this generation forever.	
8 The wicked strut about on every side	

| When vileness is exalted among the sons of men. | |

Targum

Psa. 12:1 For praise, on the lyre of eight strings. A hymn of David. [2] Redeem, O LORD, for the good are annihilated; for the faithful have ceased from the sons of men. [3] They speak lies, each to his fellow, lips are flattering; in their heart they deceive, and with a lying heart they speak. [4] The LORD will destroy from the world all flattering lips, the tongue that speaks arrogance. [5] Those who deny the essence, who say, "By our tongue we shall prevail, our lips are with us, who is our master?" [6] Because of the oppression of the poor, because of the cry of the needy, now I will arise, says the LORD; I will give redemption to my people, but against the wicked I will give testimony of evil. [7] The words of the LORD are pure words, silver purified in the furnace on the ground, refined seven times. [8] You, O LORD, will keep the righteous; you will protect them from this evil generation forever. [9] All around the wicked walk, like a leech that sucks the blood of the sons of men.

Superscript

New American Standard 1995	Hebrew
For the choir director; upon an eight-stringed lyre. A Psalm of David.	לַמְנַצֵּחַ עַל־הַשְּׁמִינִית מִזְמֹ֥ור לְדָוִֽד׃

Verse Analysis

The NASB translation is not accurate from the Hebrew. A more accurate translation is "To Him who grants victory, on the instrument with eight strings, a Psalm of David." The eight-string lyre was dedicated to the truth of redemption. In Judaism, this truth is a guarantee that the LORD's help will always be available when all human help fails. The Psalm's author was in the depths of complete mental and physical exhaustion. Nevertheless, he rises on the wings of song to regain his confidence in the LORD's saving power. His struggles knowing that the LORD's eventual help is there even when the state of human society seems hopeless.

נַצֵּחַ (natzecha) – this word means "victory." It is the name of the seventh Sefirot in the Tree of Life. Victory comes from this Sefirot freely and is always available.

Verse Rewrite Emphasizing Spiritual Awareness

To the Sefirot Netzach who grants victory, on the instrument with eight strings, a psalm of David.

Verse One

New American Standard 1995	Hebrew
Help, LORD, for the godly man ceases to be, For the faithful disappear from among the sons of men.	הוֹשִׁ֣יעָה יְ֭הוָה כִּי־גָמַ֣ר חָסִ֑יד ² ׃ כִּי־פַ֥סּוּ אֱ֝מוּנִ֗ים מִבְּנֵ֥י אָדָֽם׃

Verse Analysis

יָשַׁע (yāshaʻ) be saved, be delivered (Niphal); save, deliver, give victory, help; be safe; take vengeance, preserve (Hiphil); The first word of the verse is best translated as "save." However, an even more accurate translation is "give us new life, physically and morally."

כִּי־גָמַ֣ר חָסִ֑יד (key gamar chased) – This phrase can be translated as "has come to an end." Something has ceased to exist and to function. The phrase implies that selfless people do not exist anymore. No more cares about the people around them.

Verse Rewrite Emphasizing Spiritual Awareness

The LORD gives new life because devotion has ceased, for trustworthiness has disappeared from humankind.

Verse Two

New American Standard 1995	Hebrew
They speak falsehood to one another; With flattering lips and with a double heart they speak.	שָׁוְא יְדַבְּרוּ אִישׁ אֶת־רֵעֵהוּ שְׂפַת חֲלָקוֹת בְּלֵב וָלֵב יְדַבֵּרוּ׃

Verse Analysis

Sadly David said that people do not speak the truth to each other. A fundamental concept of a relationship between two or more persons is that everyone speaks the truth. Unfortunately, that concept seemed to be lost during this part of David's life.

חֲלָקוֹת (chalakot) – means "smooth," or "slippery." The concept of smoothness coincides with complete division or separation. It is not possible to cleave to a surface that is smooth and polished. Therefore, there is separation because a union cannot occur. Therefore, people speak smoothly polished words and figures of speech with a double heart. A double heart means that the opinions uttered are quite different from the words that are spoken.

Verse Rewrite Emphasizing Spiritual Awareness

They utter lies to each other; they speak with division words because what they say is not what they feel or believe.

Verse Three & Four

New American Standard 1995	Hebrew
May the LORD cut off all flattering lips, The tongue that speaks great things;	יַכְרֵת יְהוָה כָּל־שִׂפְתֵי חֲלָקוֹת 4 אֲשֶׁר 5 לָשׁוֹן מְדַבֶּרֶת גְּדֹלוֹת :
Who have said, "With our tongue we will prevail; Our lips are our own; who is lord over us?"	אֲמְרוּ ׀ לִלְשֹׁנֵנוּ נַגְבִּיר שְׂפָתֵינוּ אִתָּנוּ מִי אָדוֹן לָנוּ :

Verse Analysis

Eventually, the LORD will end the destruction of society because of the misuse of the spoken word. However, a social system that is based on lies will bring ruin to humankind. When this happens, evil is swathed in the clock of goodness and truth.

Verse Rewrite Emphasizing Spiritual Awareness

A day will come when the LORD will destroy the words that destroy human relationships.

On that day, our speech will only speak the truth.

Verse Five

New American Standard 1995	Hebrew
5 "Because of the devastation of the afflicted, because of the groaning of the needy, Now I will arise," says the LORD; "I will set him in the safety for which he longs."	מִשֹּׁד עֲנִיִּים מֵאַנְקַת אֶבְיוֹנִים עַתָּה אָקוּם יֹאמַר יְהוָה אָשִׁית בְּיֵשַׁע יָפִיחַ לוֹ׃

Verse Analysis

The misuse of speech to separate people will cause everyone to eke out a livelihood and existence by depriving other persons of their right to live and enjoy happiness. Some people will rise to the top of society and will force other persons to submit to them.

The second part of the verse is apocalyptic. The LORD will one day bring back happiness to everyone by eliminating the misuse of speech. After that, people will be brought together, and all persons will be equal.

Verse Rewrite Emphasizing Spiritual Awareness

Through the misuse of speech, some people control other people's lives by telling them how to live and what to do. The oppressed cry will one day invoke the LORD to bring a new life of equality for all.

Verse Six

New American Standard 1995	Hebrew
The words of the LORD are pure words; As silver tried in a furnace on the earth, refined seven times.	אִמֲרוֹת יְהוָה אֲמָרוֹת טְהֹרוֹת כֶּסֶף צָרוּף בַּעֲלִיל לָאָרֶץ מְזֻקָּק שִׁבְעָתָיִם׃

Verse Analysis

The LORD's assurance to humankind is through His words. The LORD's assurance is like a precious core of silver which is covered by ore and dross. In other words, sometimes, it is difficult to see the purity of the LORD's ways because humans have wrapped layers around them. These layers can be but are not limited to religious expressions and human doctrine. Therefore, every person's task is to see through the human part of religion and find the LORD.

Verse Rewrite Emphasizing Spiritual Awareness

The LORD's words are pure because they create binding relationships, like silver, when placed in a furnace, is refined by removing that which prevents one from seeing the silver.

Verse Seven

New American Standard 1995	Hebrew
You, O LORD, will keep them; You will preserve him from this generation forever.	אַתָּה־יְהוָה תִּשְׁמְרֵם תִּצְּרֶנּוּ ׀ מִן־הַדּוֹר זוּ לְעוֹלָם׃

Verse Analysis

The LORD always keeps his promises to humankind.

Verse Rewrite Emphasizing Spiritual Awareness

You, LORD, permanently preserve and keep your promises such a generation forever.

Verse Eight

New American Standard 1995	Hebrew
The wicked strut about on every side	סָבִיב רְשָׁעִים יִתְהַלָּכוּן כְּרֻם זֻלּוּת לִבְנֵי אָדָם׃

Verse Analysis

Rest assured that the LORD knows how to keep goodness and truth separated from evil.

Verse Rewrite Emphasizing Spiritual Awareness

Lawless people can walk among the righteous the LORD can separate them.

Complete Psalm Rewrite Emphasizing Spiritual Awareness

To the Sefirot Netzach who grants victory, on the instrument with eight strings, a psalm of David.

The LORD gives new life because devotion has ceased, for trustworthiness has disappeared from humankind.

They utter lies to each other; they speak with division words because what they say is not what they feel or believe.

A day will come when the LORD will destroy the words that destroy human relationships.

On that day, our speech will only speak the truth.

Through the misuse of speech, some people control other people's lives by telling them how to live and what to do. The oppressed cry will one day invoke the LORD to bring a new life of equality for all.

The LORD's words are pure because they create binding relationships, like silver, when placed in a furnace, is refined by removing that which prevents one from seeing the silver.

You, LORD, permanently preserve and keep your promises such a generation forever.

Lawless people can walk among the righteous the LORD can separate them.

Michael Harvey Koplitz

Psalm Thirteen

New American Standard 1995	Hebrew
13:0 For the choir director. A Psalm of David.	לַמְנַצֵּחַ מִזְמוֹר Psa. 13:1
Psa. 13:1 How long, O LORD? Will You forget me forever? How long will You hide Your face from me? 2 How long shall I take counsel in my soul, *Having* sorrow in my heart all the day? How long will my enemy be exalted over me?	לְדָוִד ׃ ²עַד־אָנָה יְהוָה תִּשְׁכָּחֵנִי נֶצַח עַד־אָנָה ׀ תַּסְתִּיר אֶת־פָּנֶיךָ מִמֶּנִּי ׃ ³עַד־ אָנָה אָשִׁית עֵצוֹת בְּנַפְשִׁי יָגוֹן בִּלְבָבִי יוֹמָם עַד־אָנָה ׀ יָרוּם אֹיְבִי עָלָי ׃ ⁴הַבִּיטָה עֲנֵנִי יְהוָה אֱלֹהָי הָאִירָה עֵינַי פֶּן־אִישַׁן הַמָּוֶת ׃ ⁵פֶּן־יֹאמַר אֹיְבִי
Psa. 13:3 Consider *and* answer me, O LORD my God; Enlighten my eyes, or I will sleep the *sleep of* death, 4 And my enemy will say, "I have overcome him," *And* my adversaries will rejoice when I am shaken.	יְכָלְתִּיו צָרַי יָגִילוּ כִּי אֶמּוֹט ׃ ⁶וַאֲנִי ׀ בְּחַסְדְּךָ בָטַחְתִּי יָגֵל לִבִּי בִּישׁוּעָתֶךָ אָשִׁירָה לַיהוָה כִּי גָמַל עָלָי ׃
Psa. 13:5 But I have trusted in Your lovingkindness; My heart shall rejoice in Your salvation. 6 I will sing to the LORD, Because He has dealt bountifully with me.	

Targum

Psa. 13:1 For praise, a hymn of David. ² How long, O LORD, will you neglect me forever? How long will you hide the splendor of your face from me? ³ How long will I put warnings in my soul, suffering in my heart daily? How long will my enemy vaunt himself over me? ⁴ Pay heed and receive my prayer, O LORD my God; illumine my eyes by your Torah, lest I sin and sleep with those who deserve death. ⁵ Lest the evil impulse should say, "I have taken control of him," [lest] my oppressors rejoice because I stray from your paths. --

⁶ But I have placed my trust in your goodness, my heart will rejoice in your redemption; I will give praise in the LORD's presence because he rewards me with good things.

Superscript

New American Standard 1995	Hebrew
13:0 For the choir director. A Psalm of David.	לַמְנַצֵּחַ מִזְמוֹר לְדָוִד׃

Verse Analysis

This psalm is usually seen as an introduction to Psalm 14. Israel appears to have been forsaken by the LORD. It's a strength as a nation is nearly exhausted. The nation fears that it may be at an end because it has come to a stage where it lacks the spiritual power to feel the presence of the LORD. Israel prays for a Divine ray of light so that it may be renewed with courage to preserve until the day when it may cause to offer a hymn of praise to the LORD thanking Him for letting the suffering bloom into happiness.

Verse Rewrite Emphasizing Spiritual Awareness

To the Sefirot Netzach who grants victory, a psalm of David.

Verse One

New American Standard 1995	Hebrew
Psa. 13:1 How long, O LORD? Will You forget me forever? How long will You hide Your face from me?	2 עַד־אָ֣נָה יְ֭הוָה תִּשְׁכָּחֵ֣נִי נֶ֑צַח עַד־אָ֓נָה ׀ תַּסְתִּ֖יר אֶת־פָּנֶ֣יךָ מִמֶּֽנִּי׃

Verse Analysis

עַד־אָ֣נָה (ad anah) - This phrase denotes a period. "How long" or "until when" are good translations of this phrase. It is the conjunction of the two words which denotes time.

עַד (ad) - translated is "often."

אָ֣נָה (anah) – translated is "where."

סָתַר verb. hide, conceal

    1. hide oneself,

    2. be hid, concealed, especially figuratively of escaping God's notice

When the LORD hides His countenance from us, the LORD is not looking upon us, and therefore, we cannot see Him. It is impossible to feel the presence of the Shekinah. It is as if the Shekinah hid from the people. The people did not want to lose the presence of the LORD.

Verse Rewrite Emphasizing Spiritual Awareness

When LORD will you forgive me forever? How long will I not be able to sense your Shekinah?

Verse Two

New American Standard 1995	Hebrew
2 How long shall I take counsel in my soul, *Having* sorrow in my heart all the day? How long will my enemy be exalted over me?	עַד־אָנָה אָשִׁית עֵצוֹת בְּנַפְשִׁי יָגוֹן בִּלְבָבִי יוֹמָם עַד־אָנָה ׀ יָרוּם אֹיְבִי עָלָי׃

Verse Analysis

If the LORD's Shekinah is not with David or Israel, the two will have to rely on their own decisions. The LORD would not help the nation determine its direction. Since the nation was not listening to the LORD through the Shekinah, why should the LORD continue to try to guide them to righteousness? So, the LORD removed the Shekinah from Israel. The psalmist grieves for the blessings that may have occurred if the Shekinah did not abandon the people.

Verse Rewrite Emphasizing Spiritual Awareness

How long must I decide life without your counsel? There is only sorrow in my heart. How long will my enemies be glad to be exalted above me?

Verse Three

New American Standard 1995	Hebrew
Psa. 13:3 Consider *and* answer me, O LORD my God; Enlighten my eyes, or I will sleep the *sleep of* death,	הַבִּיטָה עֲנֵנִי יְהוָה אֱלֹהָי הָאִירָה עֵינַי פֶּן־אִישַׁן הַמָּוֶת׃

Verse Analysis

The psalmist asks for a single ray of light to lighten and revive his soul from its state of utter mental exhaustion.

Verse Rewrite Emphasizing Spiritual Awareness

Behold and please answer me, LORD. Send a ray of light to my eyes so that I don't sleep the sleep of death.

Verse Four

New American Standard 1995	Hebrew
4 And my enemy will say, "I have overcome him," *And* my adversaries will rejoice when I am shaken.	פֶּן־יֹאמַ֣ר אֹיְבִ֣י יְכָלְתִּ֑יו צָרַ֥י יָ֝גִ֗ילוּ כִּ֣י אֶמּֽוֹט׃

Verse Analysis

If Israel did not stay strong as a nation in that period, she would have been annexed by her enemies, and thus the Jewish state would have been destroyed. If that were to happen, then the people of Israel would not perform their spiritual calling to the LORD and most likely not worship the LORD.

Verse Rewrite Emphasizing Spiritual Awareness

My enemies will say that they have beat us, and my adversaries will be happy that I am hurt.

Verse Five

New American Standard 1995	Hebrew

Psa. 13:5   But I have trusted in Your lovingkindness;
    My heart shall rejoice in Your salvation.
6   I will sing to the LORD,
    Because He has dealt bountifully with me.
	וַאֲנִי ׀ בְּחַסְדְּךָ בָטַחְתִּי יָגֵל לִבִּי
	בִּישׁוּעָתֶךָ אָשִׁירָה לַיהוָה כִּי
	גָמַל עָלָי׃

Verse Analysis

Even though it appears that the Shekinah has left the people, David remains steadfast in his trust in the LORD's lovingkindness. His heart continued to rejoice for the LORD's salvation for His people Israel.

In the NASB version verses, five and six are two verses, while in the Hebrew and Targum, they are one verse.

Verse Rewrite Emphasizing Spiritual Awareness

Yet, I still trust in Your lovingkindness, which causes my heart to rejoice through Your salvation.

Complete Psalm Rewrite Emphasizing Spiritual Awareness

To the Sefirot Netzach who grants victory, a psalm of David.

When LORD will you forgive me forever? How long will I not be able to sense your Shekinah?

How long must I decide life without your counsel? There is only sorrow in my heart. How long will my enemies be glad to be exalted above me?

Behold and please answer me, LORD. Send a ray of light to my eyes so that I don't sleep the sleep of death.

My enemies will say that they have beat us, and my adversaries will be happy that I am hurt Yet, I still trust in Your lovingkindness, which causes my heart to rejoice through Your salvation.

Psalm Fourteen

New American Standard 1995	Hebrew
⁰ *For the choir director. A Psalm of David.*	לַמְנַצֵּחַ לְדָוִד אָמַר Psa. 14:1
Psa. 14:1 The fool has said in his heart, "There is no God."	נָבָל בְּלִבּוֹ אֵין אֱלֹהִים הִשְׁחִיתוּ
They are corrupt, they have committed abominable deeds;	הִתְעִיבוּ עֲלִילָה אֵין עֹשֵׂה־
There is no one who does good.	טוֹב : ² יְהוָה מִשָּׁמַיִם הִשְׁקִיף
² The LORD has looked down from heaven upon the sons of men	עַל־בְּנֵי־אָדָם לִרְאוֹת הֲיֵשׁ
To see if there are any who understand,	מַשְׂכִּיל דֹּרֵשׁ אֶת־אֱלֹהִים : ³
Who seek after God.	הַכֹּל סָר יַחְדָּו נֶאֱלָחוּ אֵין
³ They have all turned aside, together they have become corrupt;	⁴ עֹשֵׂה־טוֹב אֵין גַּם־אֶחָד :
There is no one who does good, not even one.	הֲלֹא יָדְעוּ כָּל־פֹּעֲלֵי אָוֶן אֹכְלֵי
	עַמִּי אָכְלוּ לֶחֶם יְהוָה לֹא
Psa. 14:4 Do all the workers of wickedness not know,	קָרָאוּ : ⁵ שָׁם פָּחֲדוּ פָחַד כִּי־
Who eat up my people *as* they eat bread,	אֱלֹהִים בְּדוֹר צַדִּיק : ⁶ עֲצַת־
And do not call upon the LORD?	עָנִי תָבִישׁוּ כִּי יְהוָה מַחְסֵהוּ : ⁷
⁵ There they are in great dread, For God is with the righteous generation.	מִי יִתֵּן מִצִּיּוֹן יְשׁוּעַת יִשְׂרָאֵל
⁶ You would put to shame the counsel of the afflicted,	בְּשׁוּב יְהוָה שְׁבוּת עַמּוֹ יָגֵל
But the LORD is his refuge.	יַעֲקֹב יִשְׂמַח יִשְׂרָאֵל :
Psa. 14:7 Oh, that the salvation of Israel would come out of Zion!	
When the LORD restores His captive people,	

| Jacob will rejoice, Israel will be glad. | |

Targum

Psa. 14:1 For praise; in the spirit of prophecy through David. The fool said in his heart, "There is no rule of God on the earth." They corrupted their deeds, they despised goodness and found iniquity. There is none who does good. [2] The LORD looked down from heaven on the sons of men to see if there was any wise man seeking instruction from the presence of the LORD. [3] All alike have turned backward, they have become lax; there is none who does good, there is not even one. [4] Do they not know, all doers of falsehood? Those among my people who dine have dined on bread [and] not blessed the name of the LORD. [5] There they became afraid because the word of the LORD is in the generation of the righteous. [6] You will despise the counsel of the poor man, because he has placed his hope in the LORD. [7] Who will produce from Zion the redemption of Israel? When the LORD brings back the exile of his people, Jacob will rejoice, Israel will be glad.

Verse One

New American Standard 1995	Hebrew

The fool has said in his heart, "There is no God."
 	
     They are corrupt, they have committed abominable deeds;
     There is no one who does good.
	לַמְנַצֵּחַ לְדָוִד אָמַר נָבָל בְּלִבּוֹ
	
	 אֵין אֱלֹהִים הִשְׁחִיתוּ הִתְעִיבוּ
	
	 עֲלִילָה אֵין עֹשֵׂה־טוֹב׃

Verse Analysis

Psalm 13 voiced a faith that has sustained Israel since its inception. This faith has kept the Hebrew people together throughout its long period of destitution.

נָבָל (naval) verb, be senseless, foolish. It can also be translated as "withered." History has shown that whenever humans become foolish, they enter into a time of mental and moral degradation.

Israel's enemies called them foolish for their faith and hope in the LORD. As long as Israel kept their covenant with the LORD, they were always protected. נָבָל denotes the disappearance of unfettered moral strength. The nation was "going down the tubes," and it appeared that no one could stop it.

הִשְׁחִיתוּ הִתְעִיבוּ עֲלִילָה (hesheecheeto heteeeevoo alala) – denotes that when human actions are left unchecked, they become abominations.

Verse Rewrite Emphasizing Spiritual Awareness

To Netzach, a Sefirot of the Tree of Life by David. In his heart, the foolish man has said, "There is no God"; they are corrupt and an abomination because their activities are not those of a person who wants to do good.

Verse Two

New American Standard 1995	Hebrew
2 The LORD has looked down from heaven upon the sons of men To see if there are any who understand, Who seek after God.	יְהוָה מִשָּׁמַיִם הִשְׁקִיף עַֽל־בְּנֵי־ אָדָם לִרְאוֹת הֲיֵשׁ

Verse Analysis

Humans who deny the existence of the LORD do so because the LORD cannot be detected by reason.

Verse Rewrite Emphasizing Spiritual Awareness

The LORD observes from Heaven to find humans who are searching for Him by using their reason.

Verse Three

New American Standard 1995	Hebrew
3 They have all turned aside, together they have become corrupt; There is no one who does good, not even one.	הַכֹּל סָר יַחְדָּו נֶאֱלָחוּ אֵין עֹשֵׂה־טוֹב אֵין גַּם־אֶחָד׃

Verse Analysis

At the time of this writing, the author believed that every person was corrupt and had turned away from the LORD. Therefore, the LORD does not need to intervene and bring punishment to the people because every member of society serves as a punishment for his/her fellow citizens. In other words, the people punish each other by their violence toward each other.

There have often been periods when all humanity seemed to be corrupted, and no one does anything good.

Verse Rewrite Emphasizing Spiritual Awareness

All humanity is depraved. No one is doing anything good, not a single person.

Verse Four

New American Standard 1995	Hebrew
Do all the workers of wickedness not know, Who eat up my people *as* they eat bread, *And* do not call upon the LORD?	הֲלֹא יָדְעוּ כָּל־פֹּעֲלֵי אָוֶן אֹכְלֵי עַמִּי אָכְלוּ לֶחֶם יְהוָה לֹא קָרָאוּ׃

Verse Analysis

Even when it appears that all humanity is corrupt and perverted, there has always been a nation that respected the LORD and obeyed His divine law. That nation is Israel. Without Israel, the world would have become completely lost.

Verse Rewrite Emphasizing Spiritual Awareness

The doers of violence do not know who devours Israel like a person eating bread and has not invited the LORD?

Verse Five

New American Standard 1995	Hebrew
There they are in great dread, For God is with the righteous generation	שָׁם ׀ פָּחֲדוּ פָחַד כִּי־אֱלֹהִים בְּדוֹר צַדִּיק

Verse Analysis

פָּחֲדוּ פָחַד (gachadoo gachad) – this phrase is the verb and noun of the same word. Therefore, it means "great dread." The great dread was coming upon the people who chose not to know the LORD and preyed upon His nation Israel. These people were enslaved to their lustful desires and thus forfeited all moral freedom.

צַדִּיק (saddîq) just, lawful, righteous. The root word connotes conformity to an ethical or moral standard. צֶדֶק, then, refers to an ethical, moral standard and of course in the Old Testament, that standard is the nature and will of God. "The Lord is righteous (צַדִּיק) in all his ways and holy in all his works" (Ps 145:17).

Verse Rewrite Emphasizing Spiritual Awareness

They learned to fear the LORD because they found the LORD in the history of the righteous (Israel).

Verse Six and Seven

New American Standard 1995	Hebrew

6   You would put to shame the counsel of the afflicted,
     But the LORD is his refuge.
 	
7   Oh, that the salvation of Israel would come out of Zion!
     When the LORD restores His captive people,
     Jacob will rejoice, Israel will be glad.
	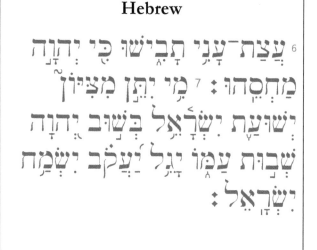

Verse Analysis

These two verses conclude the Psalm. The Jewish people have, throughout their tribulations, placed all their trust in the LORD.

Verse Rewrite Emphasizing Spiritual Awareness

You mock the counsel of the afflicted who trusts in the LORD. Who is it that extends Israel's help from Zion? One day the LORD will restore his captive people and return them from exile. Jacob will rejoice, and Israel will attain joy.

Complete Psalm Rewrite Emphasizing Spiritual Awareness

To Netzach, a Sefirot of the Tree of Life by David. In his heart, the foolish man has said, "There is no God"; they are corrupt and an abomination because their activities are not those of a person who wants to do good.

The LORD observes from Heaven to find humans who are searching for Him by using their reason.

All humanity is depraved. No one is doing anything good, not a single person.

The doers of violence do not know who devours Israel like a person eating bread and has not invited the LORD?

They learned to fear the LORD because they found the LORD in the history of the righteous (Israel).

You mock the counsel of the afflicted who trusts in the LORD. Who is it that extends Israel's help from Zion? One day the LORD will restore his captive people and return them from exile. Jacob will rejoice, and Israel will attain joy.

Michael Harvey Koplitz

Psalm Fifteen

New American Standard 1995	Hebrew

Psa. 15:0   A Psalm of David.
 	
Psa. 15:1   O LORD, who may abide in Your tent?
      Who may dwell on Your holy hill?
[2]   He who walks with integrity, and works righteousness,
      And speaks truth in his heart.
[3]   He does not slander [1]with his tongue,
      Nor does evil to his neighbor,
      Nor takes up a reproach against his friend;
[4]   In whose eyes a reprobate is despised,
      But who honors those who fear the LORD;
      He swears to his own hurt and does not change;
[5]   He does not put out his money [1]at interest,
      Nor does he take a bribe against the innocent.
      He who does these things will never be shaken.
	מִזְמוֹר לְדָוִד יְהוָה מִי־יָגוּר 1
	בְּאָהֳלֶךָ מִי־יִשְׁכֹּן בְּהַר קָדְשֶׁךָ׃ 2
	הוֹלֵךְ תָּמִים וּפֹעֵל צֶדֶק וְדֹבֵר
	אֱמֶת בִּלְבָבוֹ׃ לֹא־רָגַל עַל־ 3
	לְשֹׁנוֹ לֹא־עָשָׂה לְרֵעֵהוּ רָעָה
	וְחֶרְפָּה לֹא־נָשָׂא עַל־קְרֹבוֹ׃ 4
	נִבְזֶה בְּעֵינָיו נִמְאָס וְאֶת־יִרְאֵי
	יְהוָה יְכַבֵּד נִשְׁבַּע לְהָרַע וְלֹא
	יָמִר׃ כַּסְפּוֹ לֹא־נָתַן בְּנֶשֶׁךְ 5
	וְשֹׁחַד עַל־נָקִי לֹא לָקָח עֹשֵׂה־אֵלֶּה
	לֹא יִמּוֹט לְעוֹלָם׃

Targum

[1] A hymn of David. O LORD, who is worthy to dwell in your tabernacle, who is worthy to abide on the mountain of your sanctuary? [2] One who walks in integrity, and does righteous deeds, and speaks truth in his heart. [3] He does not slander with his tongue, he causes no harm to his fellow, and he bears no shame against his neighbor. [4] Who despises the contemptible to his face, but honors those who fear the LORD; who will swear to do harm to himself and does not change. [5] He has not given his money at interest; he has not accepted a bribe against the innocent; one who does these things will never be moved.

Verse One

New American Standard 1995	Hebrew
Psa. 15:0 A Psalm of David. **Psa. 15:1** O LORD, who may abide in Your tent? Who may dwell on Your holy hill?	1 מִזְמֹור לְדָוִד יְהֹוָה מִי־יָגוּר בְּאָהֳלֶךָ מִי־יִשְׁכֹּן בְּהַר קָדְשֶׁךָ׃

Verse Analysis

Psalm 15 briefly outlines the requirements for a human to meet with God. Such a person could enter the tent of the LORD because he/she dedicated their entire life to the House of the LORD.

גּוּר (gûr) means to abide, be gathered, be a stranger, dwell (in/with), gather together, remain, sojourn, inhabit, surely, continuing. This word is used when the journey is a short one.

One day all human beings will look to Mount Zion as the lofty center of the LORD's sanctuary on Earth.

The reference to the "tent" reminds the reader of the tent set up for the Ark of the Covenant. It sat under a tent covered with clothes until Solomon completed the LORD's house in Jerusalem.

The Holy Hill is a reference to Jerusalem.

Michael Harvey Koplitz

Verse Rewrite Emphasizing Spiritual Awareness

A Psalm of David. LORD who shall sojourn in your Tabernacle. Who will dwell on Mount Zion in Your Temple?

Verse Two

New American Standard 1995	Hebrew
2 He who walks with integrity, and works righteousness, And speaks truth in his heart.	הוֹלֵ֤ךְ תָּמִים֙ וּפֹעֵ֣ל צֶ֔דֶק וְדֹבֵ֥ר 2 אֱמֶ֗ת בִּלְבָבֽוֹ׃

Verse Analysis

הוֹלֵ֤ךְ תָּמִים֙ (holech tameem) – this phrase means a "moral way of life" which is filled with high integrity and subordinates all physical and spiritual desires without reservation to the sovereignty of the moral law. This person controls physical sensuality. According to Hebraic truth, the physical, sensual bestiality expressions cannot exist with the spiritual elevation to the LORD. The LORD drives away immoral people from His house. This person also has honest dealings with his/her fellow person. A dishonest person cannot enter the house of the LORD. This person's words are always truth.

Morality, honesty, and truthfulness constitute the threefold requirement that the Sanctuary of the LORD's Law exacts anyone who wishes to travel in it, especially for the person who wishes to dwell on Mount Zion, the holy mountain.

Verse Rewrite Emphasizing Spiritual Awareness

The person who walks in moral integrity practices righteousness and must speak the truth in his/her heart.

VerseThree

New American Standard 1995	Hebrew
[3] He does not slander [1]with his tongue, Nor does evil to his neighbor, Nor takes up a reproach against his friend;	לֹא־רָגַל ׀ עַל־לְשֹׁנוֹ לֹא־עָשָׂה לְרֵעֵהוּ רָעָה

Verse Analysis

עַל־לְשֹׁנוֹ (al-leshonu) – this phrase refers to ideas that did not emanate from the speaker's mind but that of ideas derived from other sources.

The person who can enter the Temple was to be a person of inexplicable integrity and moral honesty.

Verse Rewrite Emphasizing Spiritual Awareness

Only a perfect person who never slanders never does evil to his fellow human, nor casts blame on anyone.

Verse Four

New American Standard 1995	Hebrew

4   In whose eyes a reprobate is despised,
     But who honors those who fear the LORD;
     He swears to his own hurt and does not change;
	⁴ נִבְזֶ֨ה ׀ בְּֽעֵ֘ינָ֤יו נִמְאָ֗ס וְאֶת־יִרְאֵ֥י
	יְהוָ֥ה יְכַבֵּ֑ד נִשְׁבַּ֥ע לְ֝הָרַ֗ע וְלֹ֣א
	יָמִֽר׃

Verse Analysis

The Psalm is also referring to the interpersonal relations that every person has. These relationships are strengthened when a person lives a moral and ethical life. Relationships are built on truth. A person of high morals does not tell falsehoods about anything and especially anyone. It is this person that the LORD welcomes into His house.

Verse Rewrite Emphasizing Spiritual Awareness

The LORD does not like to see dishonorable persons. The LORD honors people who have reverence for Him. The LORD has sworn this to His people, and He does not change.

Verse Five

New American Standard 1995	Hebrew

5   He does not put out his money [1]at interest,
 	
     Nor does he take a bribe against the innocent.
 	
     He who does these things will
 	
never be shaken.
	כַּסְפּוֹ ׀ לֹא־נָתַן בְּנֶ֫שֶׁךְ וְשֹׁ֥חַד עַל־
	
	נָקִי לֹא לָקָח עֹשֵׂה־אֵלֶּה לֹא יִמּוֹט
	
	לְעוֹלָם ׃

Verse Analysis

The description of this person is unselfish toward doing good for others. Indeed, this person thrives on doing good deeds.

The reference about the bribes is because, in ancient days, judges were not paid. They made their money by accepting bribes. It was not unusual for a rich man to bribe a judge to steal his neighbors land. Therefore, it was beneficial to settle any dispute outside of the justice system of the day.

Verse Rewrite Emphasizing Spiritual Awareness

The unselfish person who loans money without interest never takes a bribe against an innocent person and always lives by this code.

Complete Psalm Rewrite Emphasizing Spiritual Awareness

A Psalm of David. LORD who shall sojourn in your Tabernacle. Who will dwell on Mount Zion in Your Temple?

The person who walks in moral integrity practices righteousness and must speak the truth in his/her heart.

Only a perfect person who never slanders never does evil to his fellow human, nor casts blame on anyone.

The LORD does not like to see dishonorable persons. The LORD honors people who have reverence for Him. The LORD has sworn this to His people, and He does not change.

The unselfish person who loans money without interest never takes a bribe against an innocent person and always lives by this code.

Michael Harvey Koplitz

Psalm Sixteen

New American Standard 1995	Hebrew
Psa. 16:0 A Mikhtam of David.	שְׁמְרֵנִי לְדָוִד מִכְתָּם Psalm 16:1
Psa. 16:1 Preserve me, O God, for I take refuge in You.	אָמַרְתְּ ² : בָךְ כִּי־חָסִיתִי אֵל
2 I said to the LORD, "You are my Lord;	בַּל־ טוֹבָתִי אַתָּה אֲדֹנָי לַיהוָה
I have no good besides You."	אֲשֶׁר לִקְדוֹשִׁים ³ : עָלֶיךָ
3 As for the saints who are in the Earth,	חֶפְצִי־כָל וְאַדִּירֵי הֵמָּה בָּאָרֶץ
They are the majestic ones in whom is all my delight.	אַחֵר עַצְּבוֹתָם יִרְבּוּ ⁴ : בָם
4 The sorrows of those who have bartered for another *god* will be multiplied;	מִדָּם נִסְכֵּיהֶם בַּל־אַסִּיךְ מָהָרוּ
I shall not pour out their drink offerings of blood,	עַל־ שְׁמוֹתָם אֶת־ אֶשָּׂא וּבַל־
Nor will I take their names upon my lips.	חֶלְקִי־מְנָת יְהוָה ⁵ : שְׂפָתָי
	גּוֹרָלִי תּוֹמִיךְ אַתָּה וְכוֹסִי ⁶ :
	אַף־ בַּנְּעִמִים לִי־נָפְלוּ חֲבָלִים
Psa. 16:5 The LORD is the portion of my inheritance and my cup; You support my lot.	אֲבָרֵךְ ⁷ : עָלָי שָׁפְרָה נַחֲלָת
6 The lines have fallen to me in pleasant places;	אַף־ יְעָצָנִי אֲשֶׁר אֶת־יְהוָה
Indeed, my heritage is beautiful to me.	שִׁוִּיתִי ⁸ : כִלְיוֹתָי יִסְּרוּנִי לֵילוֹת
	מִימִינִי כִּי תָמִיד לְנֶגְדִּי יְהוָה
Psa. 16:7 I will bless the LORD who has counseled me;	לִבִּי שָׂמַח לָכֵן ׀ ⁹ : אֶמּוֹט בַּל־
Indeed, my mind instructs me in the night.	יִשְׁכֹּן בְשָׂרִי־אַף כְּבוֹדִי וַיָּגֶל
8 I have set the LORD continually before me;	נַפְשִׁי תַעֲזֹב לֹא־ כִּי ׀ ¹⁰ : לָבֶטַח
Because He is at my right hand, I will not be shaken.	שָׁחַת לִרְאוֹת חֲסִידְךָ תִתֵּן לֹא־ לִשְׁאוֹל
	אֹרַח תּוֹדִיעֵנִי ¹¹ :

<table>
<tr>
<td>

9 Therefore my heart is glad and my glory rejoices;

My flesh also will dwell securely.

10 For You will not abandon my soul to Sheol;

Nor will You allow Your Holy One to undergo decay.

11 You will make known to me the path of life;

In Your presence is fullness of joy;

In Your right hand there are pleasures forever.

</td>
<td>

חַיִּים שֹׂבַע שְׂמָחוֹת אֶת־פָּנֶיךָ נְעִמוֹת בִּימִינְךָ נֶצַח:

</td>
</tr>
</table>

Targum

Psa. 16:1 An honest inscription of David. Protect me, O God, because I have hoped in your word. ² You have spoken – you, my soul – in the presence of the LORD. You are my God, truly my goodness is not present without you. ³ To the holy ones that are in the in the land they have declared the might of my power from the beginning; and as for those proud of their good deeds, my good will is for them. ⁴ But the wicked multiply their idols; afterwards they hurry to make their sacrifices. I will not receive favorably their libations or the blood of their sacrifices, nor will I mention their name with my lips. ⁵ The LORD is the portion of my cup and my share; you will support my lot. ⁶ The lots have fallen pleasantly for me; indeed, a beautiful inheritance is mine. ⁷ I will bless the LORD, who has counseled me; even at night my mind disciplines me. ⁸ I have placed the LORD before me always, for his presence rests on me; I shall not be shaken. ⁹ Therefore, my heart is glad, and my glory rejoices; besides, my flesh shall dwell in security. ¹⁰ For you will not abandon my soul to Sheol, you will not hand over your innocent one to see corruption. ¹¹ You will tell me the way of life; abundance of joy is in the presence of your face; pleasant things are at your right hand forever.

Superscript

New American Standard 1995	Hebrew
A Mikhtam of David.	מִכְתָּם לְדָוִד

Verse Analysis

מִכְתָּם לְדָוִד (meektam leDavid) – This phrase is translated as "a mikhtam of David" in the NASB 1995 Bible. The lexicon entry is:

"מִכְתָּם *(miktām)* **miktam.** A technical term that appears in Psalm titles. Meaning unknown.

This term is used in six Psalm titles, always linked with לְדָוִד "of" or "belonging to David" (**Ps 16** and Ps 56–59). All six are psalms of lament and four of the headings have historical references to David's struggles with the Philistines (56), Saul (57, 59) and the Arameans (60). If it comes from a root "to cover" (cf. Akkadian *katāmu*). מִכְתָּם could mean a "song of covering" or "atonement." Another view understands the term to mean an "engraving," such as an inscription on a stone slab, perhaps with gold letters (כֶּתֶם = gold)."

The Targum says "an honest inscription" of David for the superscript. Rabbi Steinsaltz uses the translation "an instruction by David."

Verse Rewrite Emphasizing Spiritual Awareness

A psalm of thanksgiving by David

Verse One

New American Standard 1995	Hebrew
Psa. 16:1 Preserve me, O God, for I take refuge in You	שָׁמְרֵנִי אֵל כִּי־חָסִיתִי בָךְ ²׃

Verse Analysis

שָׁמְרֵנִי אֵל (shameranee el) this phrase can be translated as either "preserve me" or "keep me." It refers to David's mistake that he believed that the LORD was so far away from the Earth that He would not see what was happening on Earth. Through the Bathsheba incident, David realized the mistake that he had made that the LORD was aware of his sin. After his repentance, he asked the LORD to protect him.

Verse Rewrite Emphasizing Spiritual Awareness

Hold me close to you, LORD, by allowing me to feel the presence of your Shekinah with me all the days of my life.

Verse Two

New American Standard 1995	Hebrew
2 I said to the LORD, "You are my Lord; I have no good besides You."	אָמַרְתְּ לַיהוָה אֲדֹנָי אָתָּה טוֹבָתִי בַּל־עָלֶיךָ

Verse Analysis

אָמַרְתְּ (amart) – this word can be translated as "I said." However, the term is implying much more. The term is in a feminine form of address and conveys that the person thus spoken to is weak.

David writes this Psalm as a reminder of how he should act through the rest of his life. He wanted the Shekinah to be with him and be realized that the LORD sees everything. There is no place on Earth to hide from divine justice.

טוֹבָתִי (tovatee) – can be translated as "good." It means good earthly happiness and welfare.

Verse Rewrite Emphasizing Spiritual Awareness

I said to the LORD that all my earthly goodness and welfare comes from you.

Verse Three

New American Standard 1995	Hebrew
³ As for the saints who are in the Earth, They are the majestic ones in whom is all my delight.	לִקְדוֹשִׁים אֲשֶׁר־בָּאָרֶץ הֵמָּה וְאַדִּירֵי כָּל־חֶפְצִי־בָם׃

Verse Analysis

לִקְדוֹשִׁים (leek'dosheem) – this word refers to super-terrestrial beings who are close to the LORD. It is not completely clear in the Bible who these beings are. The Watchers described in Genesis six and in the Book of the Watchers from 1 Enoch could be classified as super-terrestrial beings close to the LORD. They were angels who asked the LORD to come to the Earth and live among humans. The NASB 1995 translation is "saints who are in the earth." The Watchers would be disqualified from being these creatures. They were condemned to live on Earth, but they believed that they brought evil and despair to the world. The beings that David was speaking of is not known.

David was asking for these creatures to help him to fulfill all of his desires.

Verse Rewrite Emphasizing Spiritual Awareness

Through the holy super-terrestrial beings who are a part of the Earth, they will fulfill all my desires.

Verse Four

New American Standard 1995	Hebrew

4   The sorrows of those who have bartered for another *god* will be multiplied;
 	
    I shall not pour out their drink offerings of blood,
 	
    Nor will I take their names upon my lips.
	יִרְבּ֤וּ עַצְּבוֹתָם֙ אַחֵ֣ר מָהָ֔רוּ 4
	
	בַּל־אַסִּ֣יךְ נִסְכֵּיהֶ֣ם מִדָּ֑ם וּבַל־
	
	אֶשָּׂ֥א אֶת־שְׁמוֹתָ֗ם עַל־שְׂפָתָֽי׃

Verse Analysis

The tie of marriage illustrates the pure relationship between the LORD and humans. Each partner seeks an alliance with the other. Some people create an alliance with idols and false gods. The person who places himself/herself under the rule of the LORD will not suffer the pain that a person does who relies on idols and false gods.

Verse Rewrite Emphasizing Spiritual Awareness

About the sufferings of people who ally themselves to an idol, a false god; I will not pour out their drink offerings of blood. Nor will I speak their names.

Verse Five

New American Standard 1995	Hebrew
Psa. 16:5 The LORD is the portion of my inheritance and my cup; You support my lot.	5 יְהוָ֗ה מְנָת־חֶלְקִ֥י וְכוֹסִ֑י אַתָּ֗ה תּוֹמִ֥יךְ גּוֹרָלִֽי׃

Verse Analysis

David acknowledges that his inheritance, that is, the goodness of his life on Earth, is from the LORD. He recognizes this fact. David also acknowledges that his inheritance may make him lower than his lowest subject. That was all right because David fully surrendered to the divine will.

Verse Rewrite Emphasizing Spiritual Awareness

The LORD is the portion of my inheritance that He gives to me. I accept whatever is given to me.

Verse Six

New American Standard 1995	Hebrew
6 The lines have fallen to me in pleasant places; Indeed, my heritage is beautiful to me.	חֲבָלִים נָפְלוּ־לִי בַּנְּעִמִים אַף־ נַחֲלָת שָׁפְרָה עָלָי׃

Verse Analysis

"The lines" mean the luck that has come to David, i.e., winning a lottery. The inheritance David received was also pleasing and beautiful.

Verse Rewrite Emphasizing Spiritual Awareness

The luck that has fallen upon me is pleasant. My inheritance is also beautiful.

Verse Seven

New American Standard 1995	Hebrew
Psa. 16:7 I will bless the LORD who has counseled me; Indeed, my mind instructs me in the night.	אֲבָרֵךְ אֶת־יְהוָה אֲשֶׁר יְעָצָנִי אַף־לֵילוֹת יִסְּרוּנִי כִלְיוֹתָי:

Verse Analysis

David says that he blessed the LORD who prevented him from using the wrong path through life. David regrets the wrong paths that he took in his life.

Verse Rewrite Emphasizing Spiritual Awareness

I will bless the LORD who has given me instruction to keep me on the right path and for the nights in which my Nefesh's (flesh) desires to try to control me.

Verse Eight

New American Standard 1995	Hebrew
[8] I have set the LORD continually before me; Because He is at my right hand, I will not be shaken.	שִׁוִּיתִי יְהוָה לְנֶגְדִּי תָמִיד כִּי 8 מִימִינִי בַּל־אֶמּוֹט׃

Verse Analysis

David acknowledges his understanding that nothing on Earth is so small or insignificant that the LORD would simply ignore it.

Verse Rewrite Emphasizing Spiritual Awareness

The LORD is continually with me and seeing what I am doing. I will not be frightened that He is always at my right hand.

Verse Nine

New American Standard 1995	Hebrew
9 Therefore my heart is glad and my glory rejoices; My flesh also will dwell securely.	9 לָכֵן ׀ שָׂמַח לִבִּי וַיָּגֶל כְּבוֹדִי אַף־בְּשָׂרִי יִשְׁכֹּן לָבֶטַח׃

Verse Analysis

Again David acknowledges that all good comes from the LORD. A person can never obtain true happiness without having the LORD as a part of their lives.

Verse Rewrite Emphasizing Spiritual Awareness

Therefore my heart is glad when my glory rejoices. My Nefesh dwells in security.

Verse Ten

New American Standard 1995	Hebrew
10 For You will not abandon my soul to Sheol; Nor will You allow Your Holy One to undergo decay.	10 כִּ֤י ׀ לֹא־תַעֲזֹ֣ב נַפְשִׁ֣י לִשְׁא֑וֹל לֹֽא־תִתֵּ֥ן חֲ֝סִידְךָ֗ לִרְא֥וֹת שָֽׁחַת׃

Verse Analysis

This verse is interesting because it conveys an understanding of the Hellenistic idea of separating body and spirit. In the Near East, the idea of the spirit and body separating at death did not come until the Greek invasion. However, it appears to have been known in David's day. Alternatively, perhaps it was not known, and this Psalm was composed at a much later time and attributed to David.

Verse Rewrite Emphasizing Spiritual Awareness

You, LORD, will not abandon my Spirit to the depths of Sheol, nor will you allow your servant to undergo destruction.

Verse Eleven

New American Standard 1995	Hebrew

11 You will make known to me the path of life;
    In Your presence is fullness of joy;
    In Your right hand there are pleasures forever.
	11 תּוֹדִיעֵנִי֮ אֹ֤רַח חַ֫יִּ֥ים שֹׂ֣בַע שְׂמָח֣וֹת אֶת־פָּנֶ֑יךָ נְעִמ֖וֹת בִּימִינְךָ֣ נֶֽצַח׃

Verse Analysis

The path that the LORD placed David upon was filled with nothing but life.

Verse Rewrite Emphasizing Spiritual Awareness

You will make my path known as the path of life. In your presence is the fullness of all good things. In your right hand are pleasures forever.

Complete Psalm Rewrite Emphasizing Spiritual Awareness

A psalm of thanksgiving by David

Hold me close to you, LORD, by allowing me to feel the presence of your Shekinah with me all the days of my life.

I said to the LORD that all my earthly goodness and welfare comes from you.

Through the holy super-terrestrial beings who are a part of the Earth, they will fulfill all my desires.

About the sufferings of people who ally themselves to an idol, a false god; I will not pour out their drink offerings of blood. Nor will I speak their names.

The LORD is the portion of my inheritance that He gives to me. I accept whatever is given to me.

The luck that has fallen upon me is pleasant. My inheritance is also beautiful.

I will bless the LORD who has given me instruction to keep me on the right path and for the nights in which my Nefesh's (flesh) desires to try to control me.

The LORD is continually with me and seeing what I am doing. I will not be frightened that He is always at my right hand.

Therefore my heart is glad when my glory rejoices. My Nefesh dwells in security.

You, LORD, will not abandon my Spirit to the depths of Sheol, nor will you allow your servant to undergo destruction.

You will make my path known as the path of life. In your presence is the fullness of all good things. In your right hand are pleasures forever

Michael Harvey Koplitz

Psalm Seventeen

New American Standard 1995	Hebrew
Psa. 17:0 A Prayer of David.	תְּפִלָּה לְדָוִד שִׁמְעָה **Psa. 17:1**
Psa. 17:1 Hear a just cause, O LORD, give heed to my cry;	יְהוָה ׀ צֶדֶק הַקְשִׁיבָה רִנָּתִי
Give ear to my prayer, which is not from deceitful lips.	הַאֲזִינָה תְפִלָּתִי בְּלֹא שִׂפְתֵי
2 Let my judgment come forth from Your presence;	מִרְמָה׃ 2 מִלְּפָנֶיךָ מִשְׁפָּטִי יֵצֵא
Let Your eyes look with equity.	עֵינֶיךָ תֶּחֱזֶינָה מֵישָׁרִים׃ 3
3 You have tried my heart;	בָּחַנְתָּ לִבִּי ׀ פָּקַדְתָּ לַּיְלָה
You have visited *me* by night;	צְרַפְתַּנִי בַל־תִּמְצָא זַמֹּתִי בַּל־
You have tested me and You find nothing;	יַעֲבָר־פִּי׃ 4 לִפְעֻלּוֹת אָדָם
I have purposed that my mouth will not transgress.	בִּדְבַר שְׂפָתֶיךָ אֲנִי שָׁמַרְתִּי
4 As for the deeds of men, by the word of Your lips	אָרְחוֹת פָּרִיץ׃ 5 תָּמֹךְ אֲשֻׁרַי
I have kept from the paths of the violent.	בְּמַעְגְּלוֹתֶיךָ בַּל־נָמוֹטּוּ פְעָמָי׃
5 My steps have held fast to Your paths.	6 אֲנִי־קְרָאתִיךָ כִי־תַעֲנֵנִי אֵל
My feet have not slipped.	הַט־אָזְנְךָ לִי שְׁמַע אִמְרָתִי׃ 7
Psa. 17:6 I have called upon You, for You will answer me, O God;	הַפְלֵה חֲסָדֶיךָ מוֹשִׁיעַ חוֹסִים
Incline Your ear to me, hear my speech.	מִמִּתְקוֹמְמִים בִּימִינֶךָ׃ 8
7 Wondrously show Your lovingkindness,	שָׁמְרֵנִי כְּאִישׁוֹן בַּת־עָיִן בְּצֵל
O Savior of those who take refuge at Your right hand	כְּנָפֶיךָ תַּסְתִּירֵנִי׃ 9 מִפְּנֵי
From those who rise up *against them*.	רְשָׁעִים זוּ שַׁדּוּנִי אֹיְבַי בְּנֶפֶשׁ
8 Keep me as the apple of the eye;	יַקִּיפוּ עָלָי׃ 10 חֶלְבָּמוֹ סָגְרוּ
	פִּימוֹ דִּבְּרוּ בְגֵאוּת׃ 11 אַשֻּׁרֵינוּ
	עַתָּה סְבָבוּנִי [סְבָבוּנוּ] עֵינֵיהֶם

Hide me in the shadow of Your wings

9   From the wicked who despoil me,
My deadly enemies who surround me.

10   They have closed their unfeeling *heart*,
With their mouth they speak proudly.

11   They have now surrounded us in our steps;
They set their eyes to cast *us* down to the ground.

12   He is like a lion that is eager to tear,
And as a young lion lurking in hiding places.

Psa. 17:13   Arise, O LORD, confront him, bring him low;
Deliver my soul from the wicked with Your sword,

14   From men with Your hand, O LORD,
From men of the world, whose portion is in *this* life,
And whose belly You fill with Your treasure;
They are satisfied with children,
And leave their abundance to their babes.

15   As for me, I shall behold Your face in righteousness;
I will be satisfied with Your likeness when I awake.

יְשִׁיתוּ לִנְטוֹת בָּאָרֶץ: 12 דִּמְיֹנוֹ כְּאַרְיֵה יִכְסוֹף לִטְרוֹף וְכִכְפִיר יֹשֵׁב בְּמִסְתָּרִים: 13 קוּמָה יְהוָה קַדְּמָה פָנָיו הַכְרִיעֵהוּ פַּלְּטָה נַפְשִׁי מֵרָשָׁע חַרְבֶּךָ: 14 מִמְתִים יָדְךָ ׀ יְהוָה מִמְתִים מֵחֶלֶד חֶלְקָם בַּחַיִּים וּצְפִינְךָ [וּ][צְפוּנְךָ] תְּמַלֵּא בִטְנָם יִשְׂבְּעוּ בָנִים וְהִנִּיחוּ יִתְרָם לְעוֹלְלֵיהֶם: 15 אֲנִי בְּצֶדֶק אֶחֱזֶה פָנֶיךָ אֶשְׂבְּעָה בְהָקִיץ תְּמוּנָתֶךָ:

Targum

Psa. 17:1 A prayer of David. Accept, O LORD, my entreaty; in righteousness hear my praise; you will incline your ear to my prayer, since my lips are without guile. ² From your presence my judgment shall come forth; your eyes will behold, honesty. ³ You have tested my heart; you have visited me at night; you have purified me [and] not found corruption. [If] I thought of evil, it has not passed my mouth. ⁴ Truly, you have rebuked the deeds of the sons of men by the word of your lips; I have kept [myself from] the ways of audacity. ⁵ Support my steps in your path, lest my feet be shaken. ⁶ I have called you because you will receive my prayer, O God; incline your ear, receive my prayer. ⁷ Display your goodness, O redeemer of those who hope; from those who rise up against them by your right hand. ⁸ Guard me like the circle that is in the middle of the eye; in the shadow of your presence you will hide me. ⁹ From the presence of the wicked, those who harm me; my enemies, in the desire of their soul, surround me. ¹⁰ Their wealth has increased, their fat covers [them], their mouth has spoken arrogantly. ¹¹ Our steps now have surrounded us; their eyes are fixed to extend throughout the land. ¹² He resembles a lion who yearns to tear, or a jungle-cat that dwells in secret places. ¹³ Arise, O LORD, forestall him, strike him down; deliver my soul from the wicked man who deserves death by your sword. ¹⁴ And the righteous who hand over their souls on your account, O LORD, to death in the land, their portion is in eternal life, and their bellies will be filled with your good store; children will be satisfied, and they will leave their surplus to their children. ¹⁵ I in truth will see your countenance, I will be satisfied at the time that I awake, from the glory of your face.

Superscript

New American Standard 1995	Hebrew
Psa. 17:0 A Prayer of David.	תְּפִלָּה לְדָוִד

Verse Analysis

This Psalm is called a prayer of David. However, it is a kind of self-evaluation, the search for proper understanding before the LORD. In Psalm 16:8, David praised the lessons that occurred during the dark times in his life. This Psalm describes one of those lessons. David has come to an understanding of the difference between the righteous and their adversaries.

Verse Rewrite Emphasizing Spiritual Awareness

A self-evaluation before the LORD by David.

Verse One

New American Standard 1995	Hebrew
Psa. 17:1 Hear a just cause, O LORD, give heed to my cry; Give ear to my prayer, which is not from deceitful lips.	שִׁמְעָ֤ה יְהֹוָ֨ה ׀ צֶ֗דֶק הַקְשִׁ֥יבָה רִנָּתִ֗י הַאֲזִ֥ינָה תְפִלָּתִ֑י בְּלֹ֗א שִׂפְתֵ֥י מִרְמָֽה׃

Verse Analysis

צֶ֗דֶק (tzedek) – means "righteous." The NASB 1995 offers the translation as "just cause." The word means a condition of human affairs that is ideal to the LORD. Every human should want to live a life that is pleasing unto the LORD.

רִנָּתִ֗י (reenati) – means "cry." This word indicates a great and profound inner agitation that is invoked by joy or sadness.

David offers this prayer to the LORD, hoping that the LORD will hear his prayer. It was an honest prayer of David's condition (of his soul) when he wrote it.

Verse Rewrite Emphasizing Spiritual Awareness

Hear my thoughts of righteousness from my emotions, for I offer this prayer with the truth on my lips.

Verse Two

New American Standard 1995	Hebrew
2 Let my judgment come forth from Your presence; Let Your eyes look with equity.	מִלְּפָנֶיךָ מִשְׁפָּטִי יֵצֵא עֵינֶיךָ תֶּחֱזֶינָה מֵישָׁרִים׃

Verse Analysis

Judgment comes from the Sefirot Gevurah. David is praying to Gevurah to offer judgment. Thus, the slate would be cleared.

Verse Rewrite Emphasizing Spiritual Awareness

May the Sefirot Gevurah offer my judgment, for she will judge me fairly.

Verse Three

New American Standard 1995	Hebrew
3 You have tried my heart; You have visited *me* by night; You have tested me and You find nothing; I have purposed that my mouth will not transgress.	בָּחַנְתָּ לִבִּי ׀ פָּקַדְתָּ לַּיְלָה ³ צְרַפְתַּנִי בַל־תִּמְצָא זַמֹּתִי בַּל־ יַעֲבָר־פִּי ׃

Verse Analysis

David acknowledges that the judgment sent from Gevurah upon him was necessary as a punishment for the evil things that he did. David knows that the examination was not just of his actions but also of what was in his heart.

Verse Rewrite Emphasizing Spiritual Awareness

You have tested my heart at night; You have removed all evil from my thoughts and body so that now I am entirely cleansed and that I would not speak any evil.

Verse Four

New American Standard 1995	Hebrew
4 As for the deeds of men, by the word of Your lips I have kept from the paths of the violent.	לִפְעֻלּוֹת אָדָם בִּדְבַר שְׂפָתֶיךָ אֲנִי שָׁמַרְתִּי אָרְחוֹת פָּרִיץ:

Verse Analysis

Crimes committed against neighbors serve to bring the deeds of humans under the sovereignty of the LORD's Law to become lessons for the people who wish to be righteous. Thus evil serves the purposes of righteousness, and the criminal unwittingly advances the cause of the LORD's kingdom on earth.

Verse Rewrite Emphasizing Spiritual Awareness

The deeds of the wicked are lessons to the righteous as to how not to behave.

Verse Five

New American Standard 1995	Hebrew
5 My steps have held fast to Your paths. My feet have not slipped.	⁵ תָּמֹךְ אֲשֻׁרַי בְּמַעְגְּלוֹתֶיךָ בַּל־נָמוֹטוּ פְעָמָי :

Verse Analysis

David understood that his suffering was to become a source of strength. He asked the LORD to keep his word and actions within the bounds that the LORD's Law has drawn. The precepts of the Torah must be followed as one moves forward through their life.

Verse Rewrite Emphasizing Spiritual Awareness

My word and actions have been within the boundaries defined by your Torah.

Verse Six

New American Standard 1995	Hebrew
. **Psa. 17:6** I have called upon You, for You will answer me, O God; Incline Your ear to me, hear my speech.	אֲנִי־קְרָאתִיךָ כִי־תַעֲנֵנִי אֵל הַט־ אָזְנְךָ לִי שְׁמַע אִמְרָתִי : ⁷

Verse Analysis

David calls out to the LORD the same way a child cries out for its mother at night. The child cries out to hear the mother's voice reassuring the child that he/she is not alone. David calls to the LORD in the same manner. He needed to feel that the Shekinah was still with him.

Verse Rewrite Emphasizing Spiritual Awareness

LORD may your Shekinah assure me that You are still with me.

Verse Seven

New American Standard 1995	Hebrew
7　　Wondrously show Your lovingkindness, 　　O Savior of those who take refuge at Your right hand 　　From those who rise up *against them*.	הַפְלֵה חֲסָדֶיךָ מוֹשִׁיעַ חוֹסִים מִמִּתְקוֹמְמִים בִּימִינֶךָ ׃

Verse Analysis

One result from suffering is that the LORD offer a path to moral perfection to those who wish it through Your forgiveness. The righteous persons of this world demonstrate the trust that exists between the LORD and humanity.

Verse Rewrite Emphasizing Spiritual Awareness

Let Chesed shine forth, a help to all who trust in You because You save all who ask for it.

Verse Eight

New American Standard 1995	Hebrew
8 Keep me as the apple of the eye; Hide me in the shadow of Your wings	שָׁמְרֵנִי כְּאִישׁוֹן בַּת־עָיִן בְּצֵל כְּנָפֶיךָ תַּסְתִּירֵנִי׃

Verse Analysis

בַּת־עָיִן (bat – eyin) – literally means "daughter of my eye." This phrase is an idiom for the expression "apple of the eye." A better translation for the idiom is "the eyelid protects the eye." David was asking for the LORD's help to steer him away from the moral decay and evil in the world.

Verse Rewrite Emphasizing Spiritual Awareness

Keep me from entering into anything immoral by hiding it from me.

Verse Nine

New American Standard 1995	Hebrew
9 From the wicked who despoil me, My deadly enemies who surround me.	9 מִפְּנֵי רְשָׁעִים זוּ שַׁדּוּנִי אֹיְבַי בְּנֶפֶשׁ יַקִּיפוּ עָלָי׃

Verse Analysis

David has lost every material possession that he had. He believed that his enemies were now going to steal his soul.

Verse Rewrite Emphasizing Spiritual Awareness

The wicked who took all my possession are now are coming after my soul.

Verse Ten

New American Standard 1995	Hebrew
[10] They have closed their unfeeling *heart,* With their mouth they speak proudly.	10 חֶלְבָּמוֹ סָגְרוּ פִּימוֹ דִּבְּרוּ בְגֵאוּת׃

Verse Analysis

The Hebrew does not contain the word for "heart." A better translation is, "They have well hidden that which they cherish most, so they say proudly with their lips." David was talking about his enemies' precious possessions.

Verse Rewrite Emphasizing Spiritual Awareness

They have well hidden that which they cherish most, so they say proudly with their lips.

Verse Eleven

New American Standard 1995	Hebrew
11 They have now surrounded us in our steps; They set their eyes to cast *us* down to the ground.	11 אַשֻּׁרֵינוּ עַתָּה סְבָבוּנִי [סְבָבוּנוּ] עֵינֵיהֶם יָשִׁיתוּ לִנְטוֹת בָּאָרֶץ

Verse Analysis

David asks why his enemies hate his way of righteous living. He felt they were leading him astray from the ways of the LORD. His enemies stole his material possessions, and their present actions are directed at his way of life.

Verse Rewrite Emphasizing Spiritual Awareness

They hate our righteous living, so they try to make us stray from the right path on earth.

Verse Twelve

New American Standard 1995	Hebrew
[12] He is like a lion that is eager to tear, And as a young lion lurking in hiding places.	[12] דִּמְיֹנוֹ כְּאַרְיֵה יִכְסוֹף לִטְרוֹף וְכִכְפִיר יֹשֵׁב בְּמִסְתָּרִים׃

Verse Analysis

The enemy is ready to tear David apart like a young lion who lurks waiting for its prey.

Verse Rewrite Emphasizing Spiritual Awareness

He waits like a lion, ready to tear me apart.

Verse Thirteen

New American Standard 1995	Hebrew
Psa. 17:13 Arise, O LORD, confront him, bring him low; Deliver my soul from the wicked with Your sword,	13 קוּמָ֤ה יְהוָ֗ה קַדְּמָ֣ה פָ֭נָיו הַכְרִיעֵ֑הוּ פַּלְּטָ֥ה נַ֝פְשִׁ֗י מֵרָשָׁ֥ע חַרְבֶּֽךָ׃

Verse Analysis

David pleads with the LORD to confront his enemy and stop the wicked plan. In many places in the Hebrew Scriptures, the LORD is envisioned as a triumphant warrior with a sword.

Verse Rewrite Emphasizing Spiritual Awareness

Arise LORD and stop my enemy so my soul will not fall victim to him by using your sword.

Verse Fourteen

New American Standard 1995	Hebrew
¹⁴ From men with Your hand, O LORD, From men of the world, whose portion is in *this* life, And whose belly You fill with Your treasure; They are satisfied with children, And leave their abundance to their babes.	מְמְתִים יָדְךָ ׀ יְהֹוָה מֵמְתִים 14 מֵחֶלֶד חֶלְקָם בַּחַיִּים וּצְפִינְךָ [וּ][צְפוּנְךָ] תְּמַלֵּא בִטְנָם יִשְׂבְּעוּ בָנִים וְהִנִּיחוּ יִתְרָם לְעוֹלְלֵיהֶם ׃

Verse Analysis

מְמְתִים (mem'tim) – means "men" or "people." It denotes people of only passing importance.

וּצְפִינְךָ [וּ][צְפוּנְךָ] תְּמַלֵּא בִטְנָם (vutz'peen'cha [vu] [tz'pun'cha] t'male veet'nas] – this phrase refers to the joy to be enjoyed by the righteous people in the world to come. This joy is spiritual. Wicked people see this as something that they can steal in the physical world. They do not understand that the joy from the LORD will be available only spiritually.

It is a request to allow the wicked to believe that it is best to have all their material desires filled in this lifetime. They will not be looking for anything in the world to come. Through their actions, they will not inherit the world to come. Let them have plenty of children to leave their material wealth to because that will be their legacy.

Verse Rewrite Emphasizing Spiritual Awareness

From the men who are Your tools, O LORD; from the men of transitory import whose portion is in this life, and whose stomachs You fill with that which is hidden – let them have children in plenty and let them leave their abundance to their offspring.

Verse Fifteen

New American Standard 1995	Hebrew
15 As for me, I shall behold Your face in righteousness; I will be satisfied with Your likeness when I awake.	15 אֲנִי בְּצֶדֶק אֶחֱזֶה פָנֶיךָ אֶשְׂבְּעָה בְהָקִיץ תְּמוּנָתֶךָ :

Verse Analysis

David acknowledges that it is the spiritual joy in the world to come that is most important.

Verse Rewrite Emphasizing Spiritual Awareness

As for me, I will live in thoughts of righteousness, and one day I will awaken in your spiritual presence, and I look forward to that day.

Complete Psalm Rewrite Emphasizing Spiritual Awareness

A self-evaluation before the LORD by David.

Hear my thoughts of righteousness from my emotions, for I offer this prayer with the truth on my lips.

May the Sefirot Gevurah offer my judgment, for she will judge me fairly.

You have tested my heart at night; You have removed all evil from my thoughts and body so that now I am entirely cleansed and that I would not speak any evil.

The deeds of the wicked are lessons to the righteous as to how not to behave.

My word and actions have been within the boundaries defined by your Torah.

LORD may your Shekinah assure me that You are still with me.

Let Chesed shine forth, a help to all who trust in You because You save all who ask for it.

Keep me from entering into anything immoral by hiding it from me.

The wicked who took all my possession are now are coming after my soul.

They have well hidden that which they cherish most, so they say proudly with their lips.

They hate our righteous living, so they try to make us stray from the right path on earth.

He waits like a lion, ready to tear me apart.

Arise LORD and stop my enemy so my soul will not fall victim to him by using your sword.

From the men who are Your tools, O LORD; from the men of transitory import whose portion is in this life, and whose stomachs You fill with that which is hidden – let them have children in plenty and let them leave their abundance to their offspring.

As for me, I will live in thoughts of righteousness, and one day I will awaken in your spiritual presence, and I look forward to that day.

Michael Harvey Koplitz

Psalm Eighteen

New American Standard 1995	Hebrew
Psa. 18:0 For the choir director. A *Psalm* of David the servant of the LORD, [†]who spoke to the LORD the words of this song in the day that the LORD delivered him from the hand of all his enemies and from the hand of Saul. And he said,	פְּתַ. 18:1 לַמְנַצֵּחַ ׀ לְעֶבֶד יְהוָה לְדָוִד אֲשֶׁר דִּבֶּר ׀ לַיהוָה אֶת־דִּבְרֵי הַשִּׁירָה הַזֹּאת בְּיוֹם הִצִּיל־יְהוָה אוֹתוֹ מִכַּף כָּל־אֹיְבָיו וּמִיַּד שָׁאוּל׃ 2 וַיֹּאמַר אֶרְחָמְךָ
Psa. 18:1 "I love You, O LORD, [a]my strength."	יְהוָה חִזְקִי׃ 3 יְהוָה ׀ סַלְעִי
[2] The LORD is [a]my [1]rock and [b]my fortress and my [c]deliverer,	וּמְצוּדָתִי וּמְפַלְטִי אֵלִי צוּרִי
My God, my rock, in whom I take refuge;	אֶחֱסֶה־בּוֹ מָגִנִּי וְקֶרֶן־יִשְׁעִי
My [d]shield and the [e]horn of my salvation, my [f]stronghold.	מִשְׂגַּבִּי׃ 4 מְהֻלָּל אֶקְרָא
[3] I call upon the LORD, who is [a]worthy to be praised,	יְהוָה וּמִן־אֹיְבַי אִוָּשֵׁעַ׃ 5
And I am [b]saved from my enemies.	אֲפָפוּנִי חֶבְלֵי־מָוֶת וְנַחֲלֵי
Psa. 18:4 The [a]cords of death encompassed me,	בְלִיַּעַל יְבַעֲתוּנִי׃ 6 חֶבְלֵי
And the [b]torrents of [1]ungodliness [2]terrified me.	שְׁאוֹל סְבָבוּנִי קִדְּמוּנִי
[5] The [a]cords of [1]Sheol surrounded me;	מוֹקְשֵׁי מָוֶת׃ 7 בַּצַּר־לִי ׀
The snares of death confronted me.	אֶקְרָא יְהוָה וְאֶל־אֱלֹהַי
[6] In my [a]distress I called upon the LORD,	אֲשַׁוֵּעַ יִשְׁמַע מֵהֵיכָלוֹ קוֹלִי
And cried to my God for help;	וְשַׁוְעָתִי לְפָנָיו ׀ תָּבוֹא
He heard my voice [b]out of His temple,	בְאָזְנָיו׃ 8 וַתִּגְעַשׁ וַתִּרְעַשׁ ׀
And my [c]cry for help before Him came into His ears.	

Psa. 18:7   Then the *a*earth shook and quaked;

And the *b*foundations of the mountains were trembling

And were shaken, because He was angry.

8   Smoke went up [1]out of His nostrils,

And *a*fire from His mouth devoured;

Coals were kindled by it.

9   He *a*bowed the heavens also, and came down

With thick *b*darkness under His feet.

10   He rode upon a *a*cherub and flew;

And He sped upon the *b*wings of the wind.

11   He made *a*darkness His hiding place, *b*His [1]canopy around Him,

Darkness of waters, thick clouds of the skies.

12   From the *a*brightness before Him passed His thick clouds,

Hailstones and *b*coals of fire.

13   The LORD also *a*thundered in the heavens,

And the Most High uttered His voice,

Hailstones and coals of fire.

14   He *a*sent out His arrows, and scattered them,

And lightning flashes in abundance, and [1]routed them.

15   Then the *a*channels of water appeared,

And the foundations of the world were [1]laid bare

At Your *b*rebuke, O LORD,

At the blast of the *c*breath of Your nostrils.

הָאָ֗רֶץ וּמוֹסְדֵ֣י הָרִ֣ים יִרְגָּ֑זוּ

9 וַיִּֽתְגָּ֥עֲשׁ֗וּ כִּי־חָ֥רָה לֽוֹ׃

עָ֘לָ֤ה עָשָׁ֨ן ׀ בְּאַפּ֗וֹ וְאֵשׁ־מִפִּ֥יו

תֹּאכֵ֑ל גֶּ֝חָלִ֗ים בָּעֲר֥וּ מִמֶּֽנּוּ׃

10 וַיֵּ֣ט שָׁ֭מַיִם וַיֵּרַ֑ד וַ֝עֲרָפֶ֗ל

תַּ֣חַת רַגְלָֽיו׃ 11 וַיִּרְכַּ֣ב עַל־

כְּ֭רוּב וַיָּעֹ֑ף וַ֝יֵּ֗דֶא עַל־כַּנְפֵי־

ר֥וּחַ׃ 12 יָ֤שֶׁת חֹ֨שֶׁךְ ׀ סִתְר֗וֹ

סְבִ֥יבוֹתָ֥יו סֻכָּת֑וֹ חֶשְׁכַת־מַ֝֗יִם

עָבֵ֥י שְׁחָקִֽים׃ 13 מִ֭נֹּ֣גַהּ נֶגְדּ֑וֹ

עָבָ֥יו עָבְר֑וּ בָּ֝רָ֗ד וְגַֽחֲלֵי־

אֵֽשׁ׃ 14 וַיַּרְעֵ֬ם בַּשָּׁמַ֨יִם ׀

יְֽהֹוָ֗ה וְ֭עֶלְיוֹן יִתֵּ֣ן קֹל֑וֹ בָּ֝רָ֗ד

וְגַֽחֲלֵי־אֵֽשׁ׃ 15 וַיִּשְׁלַ֣ח חִ֭צָּיו

וַיְפִיצֵ֑ם וּבְרָקִ֥ים רָ֝֗ב וַיְהֻמֵּֽם׃

16 וַיֵּ֘רָא֤וּ ׀ אֲפִ֬יקֵי מַ֗יִם וַֽיִּגָּלוּ֮

מוֹסְד֢וֹת תֵּ֫בֵ֥ל מִגַּעֲרָתְךָ֥

יְהֹוָ֑ה מִ֝נִּשְׁמַ֗ת ר֣וּחַ אַפֶּֽךָ׃ 17

יִשְׁלַ֣ח מִ֭מָּרוֹם יִקָּחֵ֑נִי יַֽ֝מְשֵׁ֗נִי

מִמַּ֥יִם רַבִּֽים׃ 18 יַצִּילֵ֗נִי

מֵאֹיְבִ֥י עָ֑ז וּ֝מִשֹּׂנְאַ֗י כִּֽי־אָמְצ֥וּ

Psa. 18:16   He sent from on high, He took me;

He drew me out of many waters.

¹⁷   He delivered me from my strong enemy,

And from those who hated me, for they were too mighty for me.

¹⁸   They confronted me in the day of my calamity,

But the LORD was my stay.

¹⁹   He brought me forth also into a broad place;

He rescued me, because He delighted in me.

Psa. 18:20   The LORD has rewarded me according to my righteousness;

According to the cleanness of my hands He has recompensed me.

²¹   For I have kept the ways of the LORD,

And have not wickedly departed from my God.

²²   For all His ordinances were before me,

And I did not put away His statutes from me.

²³   I was also blameless with Him,

And I kept myself from my iniquity.

²⁴   Therefore the LORD has recompensed me according to my righteousness,

According to the cleanness of my hands in His eyes.

Psa. 18:25   With the kind You show Yourself kind;

מִמֶּֽנִּי ׃ ¹⁹ יְקַדְּמֽוּנִי בְיוֹם־

אֵידִי וַיְהִי־יְהֹוָה לְמִשְׁעָן לִי ׃

²⁰ וַיּוֹצִיאֵנִי לַמֶּרְחָב יְחַלְּצֵנִי

כִּי חָפֵץ בִּי ׃ ²¹ יִגְמְלֵנִי יְהֹוָה

כְּצִדְקִי כְּבֹר יָדַי יָשִׁיב לִי ׃

²² כִּי־שָׁמַרְתִּי דַּרְכֵי יְהֹוָה

וְלֹא־רָשַׁעְתִּי מֵאֱלֹהָי ׃ ²³ כִּי

כָל־מִשְׁפָּטָיו לְנֶגְדִּי וְחֻקֹּתָיו

לֹא־אָסִיר מֶנִּי ׃ ²⁴ וָאֱהִי

תָמִים עִמּוֹ וָאֶשְׁתַּמֵּר מֵעֲוֺנִי ׃

²⁵ וַיָּֽשֶׁב־יְהֹוָה לִי כְצִדְקִי

כְּבֹר יָדַי לְנֶגֶד עֵינָיו ׃ ²⁶

עִם־חָסִיד תִּתְחַסָּד עִם־גְּבַר

תָּמִים תִּתַּמָּם ׃ ²⁷ עִם־נָבָר

תִּתְבָּרָר וְעִם־עִקֵּשׁ תִּתְפַּתָּל ׃

²⁸ כִּי־אַתָּה עַם־עָנִי תוֹשִׁיעַ

וְעֵינַיִם רָמוֹת תַּשְׁפִּיל ׃ ²⁹

כִּי־אַתָּה תָּאִיר נֵרִי יְהֹוָה

אֱלֹהַי יַגִּיהַּ חָשְׁכִּי ׃ ³⁰ כִּי־בְךָ

אָרֻץ גְּדוּד וּבֵאלֹהַי אֲדַלֶּג־

With the blameless You show Yourself blameless;

26   With the pure You show Yourself pure,

And with the crooked You show Yourself astute.

27   For You save an afflicted people,

But haughty eyes You abase.

28   For You light my lamp;

The LORD my God illumines my darkness.

29   For by You I can run upon a troop;

And by my God I can leap over a wall.

Psa. 18:30   As for God, His way is blameless;

The word of the LORD is tried;

He is a shield to all who take refuge in Him.

31   For who is God, but the LORD?

And who is a rock, except our God,

32   The God who girds me with strength

And makes my way blameless?

33   He makes my feet like hinds' *feet,*

And sets me upon my high places.

34   He trains my hands for battle,

So that my arms can bend a bow of bronze.

35   You have also given me the shield of Your salvation,

And Your right hand upholds me;

And Your gentleness makes me great.

36   You enlarge my steps under me,

And my feet have not slipped.

Psa. 18:37   I pursued my enemies and overtook them,

שׁוּר : 31 הָאֵל תָּמִים דַּרְכּוֹ
אִמְרַת־יְהוָה צְרוּפָה מָגֵן
הוּא לְכֹל ׀ הַחֹסִים בּוֹ : 32
כִּי מִי אֱלוֹהַּ מִבַּלְעֲדֵי יְהוָה
וּמִי צוּר זוּלָתִי אֱלֹהֵינוּ : 33
הָאֵל הַמְאַזְּרֵנִי חָיִל וַיִּתֵּן
תָּמִים דַּרְכִּי : 34 מְשַׁוֶּה רַגְלַי
כָּאַיָּלוֹת וְעַל בָּמֹתַי
יַעֲמִידֵנִי : 35 מְלַמֵּד יָדַי
לַמִּלְחָמָה וְנִחֲתָה קֶשֶׁת־
נְחוּשָׁה זְרוֹעֹתָי : 36 וַתִּתֶּן־לִי
מָגֵן יִשְׁעֶךָ וִימִינְךָ תִסְעָדֵנִי
וְעַנְוַתְךָ תַרְבֵּנִי : 37 תַּרְחִיב
צַעֲדִי תַחְתָּי וְלֹא מָעֲדוּ
קַרְסֻלָּי : 38 אֶרְדּוֹף אוֹיְבַי
וְאַשִּׂיגֵם וְלֹא־אָשׁוּב עַד־
כַּלּוֹתָם : 39 אֶמְחָצֵם וְלֹא־
יֻכְלוּ קוּם יִפְּלוּ תַּחַת רַגְלָי :
40 וַתְּאַזְּרֵנִי חַיִל לַמִּלְחָמָה
תַּכְרִיעַ קָמַי תַּחְתָּי : 41 וְאֹיְבַי
נָתַתָּה לִּי עֹרֶף וּמְשַׂנְאַי

And I did not turn back until they were consumed.

38   I shattered them, so that they were not able to rise;

They fell under my feet.

39   For You have girded me with strength for battle;

You have subdued under me those who rose up against me.

40   You have also made my enemies turn their backs to me,

And I destroyed those who hated me.

41   They cried for help, but there was none to save,

Even to the LORD, but He did not answer them.

42   Then I beat them fine as the *a*dust before the wind;

I emptied them out as the mire of the streets.

Psa. 18:43 You have delivered me from the contentions of the people;

You have placed me as head of the nations;

A people whom I have not known serve me.

44   As soon as they hear, they obey me;

Foreigners submit to me.

45   Foreigners fade away,

And come trembling out of their ¹fortresses.

Psa. 18:46 The LORD lives, and blessed be my rock;

And exalted be the God of my salvation,

אַצְמִיתֵם ׃ 42 יְשַׁוְּעוּ וְאֵין־

מוֹשִׁיעַ עַל־יְהוָה וְלֹא עָנָם ׃

43 וְאֶשְׁחָקֵם כְּעָפָר עַל־פְּנֵי־

רוּחַ כְּטִיט חוּצוֹת אֲרִיקֵם ׃

44 תְּפַלְּטֵנִי מֵרִיבֵי עָם

תְּשִׂימֵנִי לְרֹאשׁ גּוֹיִם עַם לֹא־

יָדַעְתִּי יַעַבְדוּנִי ׃ 45 לְשֵׁמַע

אֹזֶן יִשָּׁמְעוּ לִי בְּנֵי־נֵכָר

יְכַחֲשׁוּ־לִי ׃ 46 בְּנֵי־נֵכָר

יִבֹּלוּ וְיַחְרְגוּ מִמִּסְגְּרוֹתֵיהֶם ׃

47 חַי־יְהוָה וּבָרוּךְ צוּרִי

וְיָרוּם אֱלוֹהֵי יִשְׁעִי ׃ 48 הָאֵל

הַנּוֹתֵן נְקָמוֹת לִי וַיַּדְבֵּר

עַמִּים תַּחְתָּי ׃ 49 מְפַלְּטִי

מֵאֹיְבָי אַף מִן־קָמַי

תְּרוֹמְמֵנִי מֵאִישׁ חָמָס

תַּצִּילֵנִי ׃ 50 עַל־כֵּן ׀ אוֹדְךָ

בַגּוֹיִם ׀ יְהוָה וּלְשִׁמְךָ

אֲזַמֵּרָה ׃ 51 מַגְדִּל [מִגְדּוֹל]

יְשׁוּעוֹת מַלְכּוֹ וְעֹשֶׂה חֶסֶד ׀

47   The God who executes vengeance for me,
 	
     And subdues peoples under me.
48   He delivers me from my enemies;
 	
     Surely You lift me above those who rise up against me;
 	
     You rescue me from the violent man.
49   Therefore I will give thanks to You among the nations, O LORD,
 	
     And I will sing praises to Your name.
50   He gives great deliverance to His king,
 	
     And shows lovingkindness to His anointed,
 	
     To David and his descendants forever.
	לִמְשִׁיחוֹ לְדָוִד וּלְזַרְעוֹ עַד־
	עוֹלָם׃

Targum

Psa. 18:1 For praise. About the miracles that occurred to the servant of the LORD, David, who sang in prophecy in the presence of the LORD the words of this song about all the days that the LORD delivered him from the hand of all his enemies and from the sword of Saul. **2** And he said: I will love you, O LORD, my strength. **3** O LORD, my strength and my security and the one who delivers me; the God who has chosen me has brought me near to fear him; my shield, from whose presence is given me strength and redemption over my enemies; my security. **4** David said in praise: "I pray in the LORD's presence, and from my enemies he redeems me." **5** Distress has surrounded me, like a woman who sits on the birthstool and has no strength to give birth and so is in danger of death; a band of abusive men has terrified me. **6** Armies of sinners have surrounded me; those armed with deadly weapons have confronted me. **7** When I am in distress, I pray in the presence of the LORD; and in the presence of my God I make supplication; and he accepts my prayer from his temple, and my petition in his presence is received by his ears, and is granted. **8** The earth trembled and shook and the foundations of the mountains tottered, and split, for he was angry with it. **9** The arrogance of Pharaoh went up like smoke; then he sent his anger like a burning fire that consumes before him; his rebuke burns at his utterance like coals of fire. **10** And he bent down the heavens, and his glory was manifested, a dark cloud a path before him. **11** So he was manifested in his strength over swift cherubim; and he proceeded in might on the wings of the storm-wind. **12** And he made his presence dwell in the mist, and surrounded himself with the clouds of his glory as a covering; and he made favorable rains to fall on his people, and mighty waters from the massed clouds of darkness on the wicked from the eternal heights. **13** From the splendor of his glory the clouds of heaven passed by in rebuke like the coals of fire and burning hail from his word. **14** And the LORD gave a shout from heaven, and the Most High raised up his utterance; he cast hail and coals of fire. **15** And he sent his word like arrows, and scattered them; [he sent] many lightning bolts, and confounded them. **16** And the depths of the sea became visible, and the pillars of the world were uncovered at the rebuke of the LORD, from the utterance of your mighty wrath. **17** He sent his prophets, [he who is] a mighty king who reigns in strength; he took me [and] delivered me from many Gentiles. **18** He delivered me from my enemies, for they are strong; from my foes, for they prevailed against me. **19** They confronted me in the day of my wandering; but the word of the LORD was my support. **20** And he brought me out to a broad place, he delivered me because he was pleased with me. **21** The LORD will requite me according to my merit; according to the cleanness of my hands he will answer me. **22** For I have kept the proper ways in the LORD's presence; and I have not walked in evil before the LORD. **23** For all his judgments are revealed in my sight, to do them; and his covenants I will not remove from me. 24 And I was blameless in fear of him; and I kept my soul from sins. 25 And the LORD rewarded me according to my merit; according to the cleanness of my hands in the presence of his word. 26 With Abraham, who was found pious in your presence, you showed much mercy; with his seed, Isaac, who was complete in fear of you, you completed your favorable word. 27 With Jacob, who was pure in your presence, you chose his sons from all the Gentiles, and separated his seed from all that is unfit; but with Pharaoh and his seed, and the Egyptians who thought evil thoughts against your people, you confounded them in their thoughts. 28 Because you are going to redeem the people, the house of Israel, who are esteemed among the peoples in exile; and by your word you will abase the mighty nations who prevail over them. 29 For you will light the lamp of Israel that was extinguished in the exile, for you are the lord of the light of Israel. The LORD my God will bring me out of darkness into light; he will show me his eternal consolation which is to come to the righteous. 30 For by your word I will pass through armies; and by the word of my God I will subdue mighty citadels. 31 God [is he] whose ways are true; the Torah of the LORD is pure; he is a shield to all who trust in him. 32 For because of the miracle and deliverance that you will perform for your Anointed, and for the remnants of your people who will remain, all the Gentiles, nations, and tongues will confess and say, There is no God but the LORD, for there is none besides you; and your people will say, There is none mighty except our God. 33 God, who girds on me a belt in strength, and makes blameless my way. 34 Who makes my feet like hinds'; and he will sustain me in my stronghold. 35 Who teaches my hands to do battle, and who makes my arms as strong as a bronze bow. 36 And you have given me strength and redemption; and your right hand will help me; and by your word you have multiplied me. 37 You have broadened my steps in my place, and my knee has not buckled. 38 I will pursue my enemies; [now] have I destroyed them, and I did not return until I finished them off. 39 I will destroy them, and they are unable to rise; and the slain have fallen under the soles of my feet. 40 And you have girded me with strength as a belt to do battle; you have defeated beneath me the Gentiles who rise up to do me harm. 41 And my foes you have broken in my presence; you have made them turn tail; [thus] my enemies I will destroy. 42 They seek help, but they have no redeemer; they pray in the presence of the LORD, but he does not accept their prayer. 43 I have crushed them like clods of earth before the storm-wind; and like the mud of the streets I have trodden them. 44 You will deliver me from the discords of the Gentiles; you will keep me by my destiny a benefactor at the head of the Gentiles; a people that I did not know shall worship me. 45 At the hearing of the ear, they will obey me; the sons of the peoples will desert in my presence. 46 The sons of the peoples will perish, and will go into exile from their palaces. 47 The LORD lives, and blessed is the mighty one; for from his presence strength and redemption are given to me; and exalted is God, the strength of my redemption. 48 It is God who works retribution for me, and defeats beneath me the Gentiles who arise to do me harm. [49] He delivers me from my foes; indeed against those who arise to do me harm you will make me prevail; you will deliver me from Gog and the armies of rapacious Gentiles with him. [50] Because of this, I will give praise in your presence among the Gentiles, O LORD; and I will sing praises to your name. [51] He works abundant redemption with his king, and shows favor to his Anointed, to David and his seed forever.

Spiritual Analysis

Due to the length of this psalm, it will not be presented in the same way the shorter Psalms are. In addition, a complete rewrite will not be available.

Superscript

This is a song שִׁירָה (shir) of David. He sang about the manifestations of the LORD's sovereignty, which he experienced during his lifetime. David sang to the Sefirot Netzach נִצֵּחַ (natzacha) who granted him victory over his enemies. David identifies the enemies as the agents of King Saul.

Verse 1

David uses the word אֶרְחָמְךָ (er'cham'cha), which is a love that a child feels for its mother. The Hebrew word is derived from the root word "womb." This also implies that David understood that he was a child of the LORD.

Verse 2

David recalls three distinct manifestations of the LORD's love that he experienced.

1. סַלְעִי וּמְצוּדָתִי וּמְפַלְטִי (sal'eer vum'tzudati vum'fal'ti) – "rock and my fortress and my deliverer.' David experience the LORD's protection and salvation.

2. אֵלִי צוּרִי אֶחֱסֶה־בּוֹ (aelee tzuri eachaesae bo) – "in whom I take refuge." David experienced the LORD endowing and shaping him.

3. מָגִנִּי וְקֶרֶן־יִשְׁעִי מִשְׂגַּבִּי (mageenee v'kaeraen-yeesheeeer meesaegabe) – "my shield and stronghold." David acknowledged that it is the LORD that led him during his lifetime.

Verse 3

David was versed in the history of the Israelites. He knew that the LORD has always stood by his people. Therefore, he was assured that the LORD would stand with him.

Verse 4

חֶבְלֵי־מָוֶת (chaev'lay-mavaet) "Cords of death." This poetic phrase means that death is like a cord that ultimately binds and ropes people. It can also mean the physical pains of life that surround a person. The torrents of ungodliness can be translated as "floods of wickedness terrified me." Thus it can be said that the translation of "cord of death" could be "pains of life." The pains would be the many enemies that David had throughout his lifetime. Imagine the pain David felt when his first-born son Absolam led a revolt against him.

Verse 5

This verse refers to the physical pain that David had endured. In this case, it is a physical pain that leads to death. It is at this time that David calls upon the LORD for renewed life and salvation.

Verse 6

David believed that the LORD heard his voice because he obeyed the Torah laws. Interestingly, David's soul at the time of this writing thought that he wholly followed the Torah. He did not at times. However, the Torah also says that forgiveness for sins is a part of the LORD's law. When David was challenged by the prophet Nathan about the sin with Bathsheba, David immediately repented of the sin and was punished by the child who was born from the incident died. Therefore, David believed he followed the Torah.

Verse 7

David is not describing a part of his life at this point. He mentions earthquakes because ancient people believed that these naturally occurring events resulted from the LORD showing his wrath and anger with His people.

Verse 8

The wrath of the LORD continues from verse seven. Since the cause of the commotion caused by the earthquake was not visible, the people believed that the LORD was showing His anger. It was the conduct of people that drove the LORD to reveal Himself in this manner.

Verse 9 & 10

The people believed that the LORD did intervene in earthly events. However, they could not see the LORD. The Cherub was the vehicle that the LORD used to visit the Earth to bring judgment. Therefore, it was the Sefirot Gevurah who rode on the Cherub.

Verse 11 & 12

The wrath of the LORD came about with such force that humankind was stunned. The thick clouds of the sky can block the sun's rays, thus making the day dark. Ancient people believed that they could not see the LORD on Earth because He had a hiding place. The LORD was with the Earth but was not going to reveal himself to the people at that time.

Verse 13

The love and majesty of the LORD's sovereignty would bring a new, rejuvenating future, which manifested itself in these catastrophic events.

Verse 14

It appears that the LORD shot arrows upon the Earth in a random fashion. Actually, the arrows were sent forth from the LORD with a definite goal in mind.

Verse 15

The LORD was responsible for the events described in this verse. The power of the breath of the LORD is a reminder of what happened at the Red Sea (Exodus).

The power of flooding from the sea is the same power that separated the waters to allow Israel to pass safely.

Verse 16

Even in the time of disaster David still called upon the LORD.

Verse 17

This is a parallelism of the preceding verse.

Verse 18

The calamity may have been brought by the LORD to have profound significance.

Verse 19

וַיּוֹצִיאֵנִי לַמֶּרְחָב (vayotzeeaenee lzmaer'chav) – "he brought me forth also into a broad place." David thanked the LORD for removing those obstacles that confined him during his life journey.

Verse 20

David expressed his loyalty to the LORD. It did not matter what calamity befell David; he never lost his love and commitment to the ways of the LORD.

Verse 21

David kept his attention upon the pathway laid out by the LORD. He tried to do what was right in the eyes of the LORD.

Verse 22

David said that he lived by the definition that the LORD established for social relationships. It could be argued that David was not 100% following the principles. How could David say that he followed the laws about social relationships after the Bathsheba incident? Therefore, it is possible that David penned this psalm before he was king. The superscript says that the psalm was written while Saul was pursuing David. Therefore, the Bathsheba incident had not occurred yet.

Verse 23

David believed that he was keeping himself from sin only because he clung to the LORD. He felt that the LORD was close to him because he mastered his inequity.

Verse 24

David felt the rewards of righteousness. The LORD did not allow Saul's men to find David and kill him. The cleanness of his hands was the sinless David.

Verse 25 & 26

There are three degrees of character.

1. The positive expression of complete, selfless devotion to the service of the LORD and the welfare of His world.
2. The complete subordination of the entire personality to the rule of Divine Law.
3. A person who is still in the process of perfecting him/herself.

The LORD reveals Himself to each person in accordance with their character.

Verse 27

David recognized how the LORD appears to humankind. Saving the afflicted people is one way.

Verse 28

The psalm returns to being focused on David. He wants the LORD to illuminate his path, so he does not walk into darkness. The darkness represents sin.

Verse 29

David acknowledges that his courage comes from the LORD.

Verse 30

The LORD reveals Himself to His people through his acts. The LORD remains constant for a reason, for His acts are always the same. It is the diversity of human conduct that the LORD's discipline seems to be different. However, the Sefirot Gevurah always judges in the same manner.

Verse 31

Only the LORD can stop the suffering that had been brought down from Heaven. The acts of the Sefirot Gevurah can be halted by the Sefirot Chesed.

Verse 32

David acknowledges that the LORD gave him the strength to combat his enemies with victory. This is the same force that guided his life to moral perfection.

Verse 33 & 34

It is the LORD who trained David to win the war against his enemies.

Verse 35

Now that David had been trained for battle by the LORD, He gave David the shield of salvation. The LORD entrusted David with the task of bringing to Israel the protection and salvation that was promised to the people.

Verse 36

The LORD called David into a position in public life dedicated to the common welfare of the people. Through the LORD's aid to David, he had the strength to do the job without stumbling or swaying.

Verses 37-39

David acknowledged that because of the LORD's help, he was able to destroy his enemies. David believed that his enemies would have intentionally ruined Israel. He probably thought that his enemies would turn Israel away from the LORD and to the pagan gods of the neighboring countries.

Verses 40-42

Not only would the LORD give David victory over his enemies from outside his court, He also gave him victory over the enemies that were lurking in his court. When David defeated an enemy, that enemy would not be able to rise again to challenge him. This would include family members seeking revenge.

Verses 43 & 44

Foreigners who only knew about David by reputation were willing to submit to his commands. David recognized that some of his enemies would conceal their hatred so that they could reap the rewards of being a false friend.

Verse 45

A time would come when David would not have to go to war. Peace existed in Israel, and security was obtained.

Verse 46

David acknowledged that even after the wars are complete and an objective of the LORD's has been achieved, the LORD will still continue to bless his life and be with him.

Verse 47 & 48

This is a repetition of an earlier David statement. David knew that the LORD was always with him. Even after David's victory, the LORD would not leave him, and he knew this.

Verse 49

David envisioned a peaceful future with a dedication to the LORD that should never end.

Verse 50

David received loving kindness from the Sefirot Chesed all the days of his life. David also asked that Chesed would be with his descendants.

Psalm Nineteen

New American Standard 1995	Hebrew

Psa. 19:0 For the choir director. A Psalm of David.
 	
Psa. 19:1 The *ᵃ*heavens are telling of the glory of God;
    And their *ᵇ*expanse is declaring the work of His hands.
2   Day to *ᵃ*day pours forth speech,
    And *ᵇ*night to night reveals knowledge.
3   There is no speech, nor are there words;
    Their voice is not heard.
4   Their *¹ᵃ*line has gone out through all the earth,
    And their utterances to the end of the world.
    In them He has *ᵇ*placed a tent for the sun,
5   Which is as a bridegroom coming out of his chamber;
    It rejoices as a strong man to run his course.
6   Its *ᵃ*rising is from *¹*one end of the heavens,
    And its circuit to the *²*other end of them;
    And there is nothing hidden from its heat.
 	
Psa. 19:7 *ᵃ*The law of the LORD is *¹ᵇ*perfect, *ᶜ*restoring the soul;
    The testimony of the LORD is *ᵈ*sure, making *ᵉ*wise the simple.
	Psa. 19:1 לַמְנַצֵּחַ מִזְמֹור
	לְדָוִד : ² הַשָּׁמַיִם מְסַפְּרִים
	כְּבֹוד־אֵל וּמַעֲשֵׂה יָדָיו
	מַגִּיד הָרָקִיעַ : ³ יֹום לְיֹום
	יַבִּיעַ אֹמֶר וְלַיְלָה לְּלַיְלָה
	יְחַוֶּה־דָּעַת : ⁴ אֵין־אֹמֶר
	וְאֵין דְּבָרִים בְּלִי נִשְׁמָע
	קֹולָם : ⁵ בְּכָל־הָאָרֶץ ׀ יָצָא
	קַוָּם וּבִקְצֵה תֵבֵל מִלֵּיהֶם
	לַשֶּׁמֶשׁ שָׂם־אֹהֶל בָּהֶם : ⁶
	וְהוּא כְּחָתָן יֹצֵא מֵחֻפָּתֹו
	יָשִׂישׂ כְּגִבֹּור לָרוּץ אֹרַח : ⁷
	מִקְצֵה הַשָּׁמַיִם ׀ מֹוצָאֹו
	וּתְקוּפָתֹו עַל־קְצֹותָם וְאֵין
	נִסְתָּר מֵחַמָּתֹו : ⁸ תֹּורַת
	יְהוָה תְּמִימָה מְשִׁיבַת נָפֶשׁ
	עֵדוּת יְהוָה נֶאֱמָנָה מַחְכִּימַת
	פֶּתִי : ⁹ פִּקּוּדֵי יְהוָה יְשָׁרִים
	מְשַׂמְּחֵי־לֵב מִצְוַת יְהוָה

8   The precepts of the LORD are
^aright, ^brejoicing the heart;

    The commandment of the LORD
is ^cpure, ^denlightening the eyes.

9   The fear of the LORD is clean,
enduring forever;

    The judgments of the LORD are
^atrue; they are ^brighteous altogether.

10   They are more desirable than
^agold, yes, than much fine gold;

    ^bSweeter also than honey and the
drippings of the honeycomb.

11   Moreover, by them ^aYour servant
is warned;

    In keeping them there is great
^breward.

12   Who can ^adiscern *his* errors?
^bAcquit me of ^chidden *faults.*

13   Also keep back Your servant
^afrom presumptuous *sins;*

    Let them not ^brule over me;

    Then I will be ^{1c}blameless,

    And I shall be acquitted of ^dgreat
transgression.

14   Let the words of my mouth and
^athe meditation of my heart

    Be acceptable in Your sight,

    O LORD, ^bmy rock and my
^cRedeemer.

בָּרָה מְאִירַת עֵינָיִם׃ 10

יִרְאַת יְהֹוָה ׀ טְהוֹרָה עוֹמֶדֶת
לָעַד מִשְׁפְּטֵי־יְהֹוָה אֱמֶת

צָדְקוּ יַחְדָּו׃ 11 הַנֶּחֱמָדִים

מִזָּהָב וּמִפַּז רָב וּמְתוּקִים

מִדְּבַשׁ וְנֹפֶת צוּפִים׃ 12 גַּם־

עַבְדְּךָ נִזְהָר בָּהֶם בְּשָׁמְרָם

עֵקֶב רָב׃ 13 שְׁגִיאוֹת מִי־

יָבִין מִנִּסְתָּרוֹת נַקֵּנִי׃ 14 גַּם

מִזֵּדִים ׀ חֲשֹׂךְ עַבְדֶּךָ אַל־

יִמְשְׁלוּ־בִי אָז אֵיתָם וְנִקֵּיתִי

מִפֶּשַׁע רָב׃ 15 יִהְיוּ לְרָצוֹן ׀

אִמְרֵי־פִי וְהֶגְיוֹן לִבִּי לְפָנֶיךָ

יְהֹוָה צוּרִי וְגֹאֲלִי׃

References

Psalm 19:1
[a]Ps 8:1; 50:6; Rom 1:19, 20
[b]Gen 1:6, 7

Psalm 19:2
[a]Ps 74:16
[b]Ps 139:12

Psalm 19:4
[1]Another reading is *sound*
[a]Rom 10:18
[b]Ps 104:2

Psalm 19:6
[1]Lit *the*
[2]Lit *the ends*
[a]Ps 113:3; Eccl 1:5

Psalm 19:7
[1]I.e. blameless
[a]Ps 111:7
[b]Ps 119:160
[c]Ps 23:3
[d]Ps 93:5
[e]Ps 119:98-100

Psalm 19:8
[a]Ps 119:128
[b]Ps 119:14
[c]Ps 12:6
[d]Ps 36:9

Psalm 19:9
[a]Ps 119:142
[b]Ps 119:138

Psalm 19:10

[a]Ps 119:72, 127
[b]Ps 119:103

Psalm 19:11
[a]Ps 17:4
[b]Ps 24:5, 6; Prov 29:18

Psalm 19:12
[a]Ps 40:12; 139:6
[b]Ps 51:1, 2
[c]Ps 90:8; 139:23, 24

Psalm 19:13
[1]Lit *complete*
[a]Num 15:30
[b]Ps 119:133
[c]Ps 18:32
[d]Ps 25:11

Psalm 19:14
[a]Ps 104:34
[b]Ps 18:2
[c]Ps 31:5; Is 47:4

Targum

[1] For praise; a psalm of David. [2] Those who behold, the heavens tell of the glory of the LORD; those who gaze at the sky recount the works of his hands. [3] Day to day tells more of the word; but night to night tells less knowledge. [4] There is no utterance of complaint, and there are no words of confusion, for their voice is not heard. [5] The line of their conversation reaches through the whole earth, and their words to the end of the world. In them [the heavens] he placed a splendid dwelling for the sun. [6] And he, in the morning, when he comes forth, will come forth like a groom who comes out of his canopy, and in splendor will rejoice like a warrior to run the course. [7] His rising is at the ends of the earth, and his might reaches to all their edges; and there is none who can hide from his heat. [8] The Torah of the LORD is perfect, restoring the soul; the testimony of the LORD is reliable, making wise the fool. [9] The commands of the LORD are upright, gladdening the heart; the command of the LORD is bright, enlightening the eyes. [10] The fear of the LORD is pure, lasting forever; the judgments of the LORD are faithfulness; they are altogether just. [11] More desirable than gold or than much fine gold; and more pleasant than honey or the sweet honeycombs. [12] Truly, your servant has been careful for them, to observe them; because of this, he was made ruler of Israel. [13] Who knows unwitting sins? And from secret faults make me innocent. [14] Truly, from the arrogant deliver your servant, that they may not rule over me; then I will be without blemish, and I will be innocent of great sin. [15] Let the utterances of my mouth and the thought of my mind be acceptable in your presence, O LORD, my strength and my redeemer.

Spiritual Analysis

The spiritual rewrites for the verses are in bold.

Introduction to the Psalm

The psalmist refers to the flawless precision in the sky as the manifestation of the infinite wisdom and power of the Creation. Even with all its flawlessness to fully reveal the LORD, the Torah must be studied. The sage Malbim said that a diligent scholar who is on a quest for the LORD would be assisted by a holy spirit that resembles a prophecy. The psalmist offers six ways that the comprehension of the LORD is gained through Torah scholarship. The Torah also revealed how sin warped humans, and only Torah study can make humanity right once again.

Superscript (verse zero)

To the Sefirah Netzach who offers me victory.

Verse One

David says that any person who examines the nature of Heaven and Earth will know that there is a God. Heaven, especially the expanse, is flawless. The stars and planets move in patterns that never differ. Ancient people believed that the LORD was sending them a message when something different occurs, like a comet. Without light pollution, ancient people were able to see more of the sky at night. The connection between the firmament and the Torah is that the Torah was the blueprint of the Universe. Thus to understand the firmament, the Torah must be studied.

The firmament tells us about the works of the LORD, and the expanse (the stars and planet) show us His creation.

Verse Two

The daytime is when the glory of the LORD is expressed. During the night, new understandings and learnings about the LORD occur. The night reveals the quasi-Sefirot Da'at because the knowledge of the Godhead is revealed.

לַיְלָה לְּלַיְלָה (lay'la l'layla) – "night to night." This phrase emphasizes the idea that knowledge received from Da'at in the evening is added to every night. An old set of sayings are: "rise and serve the Word," and the other is "lie down in peace; there Da'at watches over you."

Day by day I hear speech, and night by night reveals Da'at

Verse three

The day itself cannot talk. The psalmist is saying the day exists, and we can learn about the LORD in it.

There is no talk, nor words; you cannot hear the voice of the day

Verse four

The measuring line refers to laying out a measuring line to stake off territory for a purpose. In this case, the heavens assign and set the bounds for the development of every creature on the Earth. It was believed that a chariot pulled the sun across the sky (this idea is strongly expressed in 1 Enoch). The line could be where the horizon meets the Earth. The sun was pulled in its chariot from one horizon to the opposite.

When the sun went down, the people believed it was placed in a tent until the next day.

The measuring line defines the horizons, where the world of man begins and ends; in this space, their words speak. The LORD has set up a tent for the sun to rest when it is not shining on the Earth.

Verse five & six

Like a bridegroom implies that the sun rejoices when it comes "out" every day, it has tremendous power, but it cannot choose its won point of origin or its orbit. The Holy Scriptures guide humans to the fulfillment of life's tasks within the framework of the constellation of existence that the LORD established.

The sun is like a bridegroom ready to be wed; the sun rejoices about its power, but it must follow the course established for it.

Even with such power, the sun must stay in its designated place in the Heavens and complete its orbit that the LORD has determined for it.

Verse 7

The psalmist turns to the Torah. If humans keep their concerns on spirituality, they will better understand the language of Heaven and Earth and its place in the world which the LORD rules. The divine Law, written in the Torah, controls the Universe. Since the LORD wrote the Torah, it is the LORD's words that control everything.

The Torah is all-encompassing and will respond to the human soul; the LORD is faithful and brings wisdom to the inexperienced person.

Verse Eight

The LORD has given humans several mandates: orders and obligations on living in the terrestrial world. The mandates are given to humans to help us live properly and enter relationships with the LORD and each other. They are not laws to hinder humanity but rather laws to free us to live a life worthy to the LORD.

The mandates of the LORD are for us to live well; the mandates rejoice the heart because the commandment of the LORD is brilliant and enlightening to the eyes.

The mandates of the LORD are upright; they cause the heart to rejoice because the commandments are brilliant and enlightening to the eyes.

Verse Nine

The English translation uses the word "fear." This word can be translated as "reverence." If one enters the LORD's presence, a sense of reverence and fear should come to the person immediately. The acts of Gevurah (judgment) are given to humanity to help humanity learn the ways of the LORD as defined in the Torah. The consequences can be viewed as a punishment or a correction To the society's norms of the day.

Reverence of the LORD is pure and endures forever; Gevurah consistently demonstrates mercy and tolerance. Sometimes the judgment from Gevuah seems harsh, but it is that way to teach the people a needed-to-know lesson.

Have pure reverence of the LORD; enduring forever, because the ways of Geruvah always have a touch of Chesed.

Verse 10

For the spiritually-minded person, the treasures of Heaven are far more critical than the treasures of the Earth. Humans tend to want an accumulation of materialism, and they use this material to show other people their worth. That may work fine on the planet; however, in Heaven these material objects do not exist. Therefore which is more important to collect, spiritual treasures or earthly treasures?

The purity of the LORD is more desirable than gold and the finest gems, definitely sweeter than honey or the finest nectar.

Verse 11

David knew that the Laws of the LORD restrained him from doing some things that he wanted to do. As he gained wisdom, he realized that it was best to follow the Law than his carnal instincts.

Your servant knew of your Laws, and by keeping them, he recognized the rich rewards.

Verse 12

David was concerned about the errors that he committed because he did not have a perfect understanding of what the LORD expected of him

Who can discern errors? Who cleans me from hidden faults.

Verse 13

David asked the LORD to protect him from errors he made because of his lack of understanding and those errors created by the evil principles of depraved men who might influence him in times of weaknesses.

Prevent your servant from committing wins acts so the acts do not rule over me; then I will be blameless and innocent of sins.

Verse 14

David asks the LORD to listen to him and give him His attention.

May the words I speak, and the meditation of my heart find favor before You, my rock and my Redeemer.

Complete Psalm Rewrite Emphasizing Spiritual Awareness

To the Sefirah Netzach who offers me victory.

The firmament tells us about the works of the LORD, and the expanse (the stars and planet) show us His creation.

Day by day I hear speech, and night by night reveals Da'at

There is no talk, nor words; you cannot hear the voice of the day

The measuring line defines the horizons, where the world of man begins and ends; in this space, their words speak. The LORD has set up a tent for the sun to rest when it is not shining on the Earth.

The sun is like a bridegroom ready to be wed; the sun rejoices about its power, but it must follow the course established for it.

Even with such power, the sun must stay in its designated place in the Heavens and complete its orbit that the LORD has determined for it.

The Torah is all-encompassing and will respond to the human soul; the LORD is faithful and brings wisdom to the inexperienced person.

The mandates of the LORD are upright; they cause the heart to rejoice because the commandments are brilliant and enlightening to the eyes.

Have pure reverence of the LORD; enduring forever, because the ways of Geruvah always have a touch of Chesed.

The purity of the LORD is more desirable than gold and the finest gems, definitely sweeter than honey or the finest nectar.

Your servant knew of your Laws, and by keeping them, he recognized the rich rewards.

Who can discern errors? Who cleans me from hidden faults.

Prevent your servant from committing wins acts so the acts do not rule over me; then I will be blameless and innocent of sins.

May the words I speak, and the meditation of my heart find favor before You, my rock and my Redeemer.

Psalm Twenty

New American Standard 1995	Hebrew
Psa. 20:0 For the choir director. A Psalm of David.	‏לַמְנַצֵּחַ מִזְמוֹר לְדָוִד ׃ Psa. 21:1 2
Psa. 20:1 May the LORD answer you *a*in the day of trouble!	‏יְהוָה בְּעָזְּךָ יִשְׂמַח־מֶלֶךְ
May the *b*name of the *c*God of Jacob set you *securely* on high!	‏וּבִישׁוּעָתְךָ מַה־יָּגֶיל [יָּגֶל]
2 May He send you help *a*from the sanctuary	‏מְאֹד ׃ 3 תַּאֲוַת לִבּוֹ נָתַתָּה לּוֹ
And *b*support you from Zion!	‏וַאֲרֶשֶׁת שְׂפָתָיו בַּל־מָנַעְתָּ
3 May He *a*remember all your meal offerings	‏סֶּלָה ׃ 4 כִּי־תְקַדְּמֶנּוּ בִּרְכוֹת
And *b*find your burnt offering ¹acceptable! ²Selah.	‏טוֹב תָּשִׁית לְרֹאשׁוֹ עֲטֶרֶת פָּז ׃ 5
	‏חַיִּים ׀ שָׁאַל מִמְּךָ נָתַתָּה לּוֹ
Psa. 20:4 May He grant you your *a*heart's desire	‏אֹרֶךְ יָמִים עוֹלָם וָעֶד ׃ 6 גָּדוֹל
And *b*fulfill all your ¹counsel!	‏כְּבוֹדוֹ בִּישׁוּעָתֶךָ הוֹד וְהָדָר
5 ¹We will *a*sing for joy over your ²victory,	‏תְּשַׁוֶּה עָלָיו ׃ 7 כִּי־תְשִׁיתֵהוּ
And in the name of our God we will *b*set up our banners.	‏בְרָכוֹת לָעַד תְּחַדֵּהוּ בְשִׂמְחָה
May the LORD *c*fulfill all your petitions.	‏אֶת־פָּנֶיךָ ׃ 8 כִּי־הַמֶּלֶךְ בֹּטֵחַ
	‏בַּיהוָה וּבְחֶסֶד עֶלְיוֹן בַּל־
Psa. 20:6 Now *a*I know that the LORD saves His anointed;	‏יִמּוֹט ׃ 9 תִּמְצָא יָדְךָ לְכָל־
He will *b*answer him from His holy heaven	‏אֹיְבֶיךָ יְמִינְךָ תִּמְצָא שֹׂנְאֶיךָ ׃ 10
With the ¹c*saving strength of His right hand.	‏תְּשִׁיתֵמוֹ ׀ כְּתַנּוּר אֵשׁ לְעֵת
7 Some ¹*boast* in chariots and some in *a*horses,	‏פָּנֶיךָ יְהוָה בְּאַפּוֹ יְבַלְּעֵם
But *b*we ²will boast in the name of the LORD, our God.	‏וְתֹאכְלֵם אֵשׁ ׃ 11 פִּרְיָמוֹ מֵאֶרֶץ
	‏תְּאַבֵּד וְזַרְעָם מִבְּנֵי אָדָם ׃ 12
	‏כִּי־נָטוּ עָלֶיךָ רָעָה חָשְׁבוּ
	‏מְזִמָּה בַּל־יוּכָלוּ ׃ 13 כִּי

8   They have ^abowed down and fallen,
 	
       But we have ^brisen and stood upright.
9   ^{1a}Save, O LORD;
 	
       May the ^bKing answer us in the
 	
day we call.
	תִּשִׁיתֵמוֹ שֶׁכֶם בְּמֵיתָרֶיךָ תְּכוֹנֵן
	עַל־פְּנֵיהֶם ׃ ¹⁴ רוּמָה יְהוָה
	בְעֻזֶּךָ נָשִׁירָה וּנְזַמְּרָה
	גְּבוּרָתֶךָ ׃

References

Psalm 20:1
[a]Ps 50:15
[b]Ps 91:14
[c]Ps 46:7, 11

Psalm 20:2
[a]Ps 3:4
[b]Ps 110:2

Psalm 20:3
[1]Lit *fat*
[2]*Selah* may mean: *Pause, Crescendo* or *Musical interlude*
[a]Acts 10:4
[b]Ps 51:19

Psalm 20:4
[1]Or *purpose*
[a]Ps 21:2
[b]Ps 145:19

Psalm 20:5
[1]Or *Let us sing*
[2]Or *salvation*
[a]Ps 9:14
[b]Ps 60:4
[c]1 Sam 1:17

Psalm 20:6
[1]Or *mighty deeds of the victory of His right hand*
[a]Ps 41:11
[b]Is 58:9
[c]Ps 28:8

Psalm 20:7
[1]Or praise *chariots,* or trust, or are strong *through*
[2]Lit *make mention of;* or *praise the name*
[a]Ps 33:17
[b]2 Chr 32:8

Psalm 20:8
[a]Is 2:11, 17
[b]Ps 37:24; Mic 7:8

Psalm 20:9
[1]Or *O LORD,* save the king; answer us
[a]Ps 3:7
[b]Ps 17:6

Targum

Psa. 20:1 For praise; a psalm of David. [2] May the LORD receive your prayer in the day of trouble, may the name of the God of Jacob lift you up. [3] May he send your help from his sanctuary, and from Zion give you aid. [4] May he remember all your offerings, and may your whole-offerings drip with fat forever. [5] May he give you according to your desires, and may he fulfill all your counsel. [6] Your people will say, "Let us give praise for your redemption, and in the name of our God we will be mustered; may the LORD fulfill all your requests." [7] Now I know that the LORD has redeemed his anointed; he has accepted his prayer from his holy dwelling in the heavens; in might is the redemption of his right hand. [8] Some by chariots, and some by horses, but we will swear by the name of the LORD our God. [9] They have stooped and fallen, but we have remained upright and become strong. [10] O LORD, redeem us, mighty king, accept our prayer in the day we call out.

Spiritual Analysis

The spiritual rewrites for the verses are in bold.

Introduction

This Psalm is the response of the people of Israel to Psalm 19. In that Psalm, David expressed his loyalty to the LORD's Law. The Psalm is addressed to David, proclaiming that they too have come to understand his relationship with the LORD. They wish to offer him their sentiments of loyalty and affection.

Superscript

לַמְנַצֵּחַ (lam'nazecha) – the English translations of this Psalm like to use the phrase "for the choir director," however this translation is inaccurate. The "Theological Wordbook of the Old Testament" indicates that this translation is far from correct. A proper translation is "To Netzach." The Sefirah Netzach offers victory when its light is placed upon a person. The implication is that the people are happy that David had so many military victories. When David was victorious, the people were protected and prospered. The people are offering this prayer about David and their allegiance to him and the Sefirot Netzach.

To the Sefirot Netzach, a psalm of David.

Verse One

The "day of trouble" is a time of dire circumstances of inevitable disaster. Jacob is called out because every time it appeared that Jacob was in the day of trouble, the

LORD saved him. The LORD will protect and assist any person who upholds the Laws and Mitzvot of the Torah.

The LORD will answer you in the days of trouble; the name of the God of Jacob will raise you on high.

Verse Two

It is believed that our spiritual foundation and strength come to humans through Mount Zion, the location of the LORD's Temple. The Zohar speaks about places on the Earth where the goodness of the Sefirot flows into Malchut (our realm). One of these places is Mount Zion in Israel. There are other locations around the world. However, the most active place is Mount Zion. The help and support from Zion are to help each of us to come closer to the LORD.

Your spiritual help will come from His Sanctuary, and spiritual strength to resist evil will come from Zion.

Verse Three

The meal offering is symbolic of the joy of life, thus symbolizing a person's entire fate. It can be said that this offering is giving back to the LORD some of the joys and blessings that have been bestowed. By doing this, the person demonstrates their dependence on the LORD. The burnt offerings are another example of an understanding of the blessings from the LORD.

The LORD will accept your offerings of homage and will always find your offerings, your thanksgiving, acceptable. Meditate on this verse.

Verse Four

The people are saying to David that they will lay down all desires to what the LORD wants. They saw how David reacted to the LORD and tried to live a life worthy of the LORD's name. In return, the LORD gave David all of his heart's desires.

May the LORD give you everything your heart desires and always be your guide in life.

Verse Five

The people rejoiced because David the Sefirot Netzach showered him with blessings. They set up banners that allowed them to rally around the various blessings. Therefore, the banners represented each blessing.

We will shout for joy every time Netzach blesses you by rallying around your banner in the name of the LORD; may Netzach fulfill all your desires through victory.

Verse Six

The people saw that the LORD was with David throughout his troubles and triumphs. Even when David sinned, the LORD was with him. The LORD gave David a method to offer repentance. The people experienced the LORD with David.

Now I have come to know that the LORD has granted happiness to his appointed king (David); He will always hear you and will answer you from the Heavens and his acts of salvation of His right hand will sustain you.

Verse Seven

The people will always remember the LORD by His holy name. Other nations know their god in chariots and horse. Israel will not worship material things as the LORD.

Other nations see their god in chariots and others in horses, but for us, we remember our LORD by His holy name.

Verse Eight

The other nations who celebrate their god have fallen and stayed down while we have always risen and stood upright because the LORD is our God and takes care of His children.

When other nations fell, not to rise again, we have fallen, but the LORD raises us, and we will stay risen.

Verse Nine

The people's confidence was in the Divine aid that the LORD offered, and the people will always consider the LORD a king.

May the LORD grant salvation to his people. The King God will answer us on the days which we call upon Him.

Complete Psalm Rewrite Emphasizing Spiritual Awareness

To the Sefirot Netzach, a psalm of David.

The LORD will answer you in the days of trouble; the name of the God of Jacob will raise you on high.

Your spiritual help will come from His Sanctuary, and spiritual strength to resist evil will come from Zion.

The LORD will accept your offerings of homage and will always find your offerings, your thanksgiving, acceptable. Meditate on this verse.

May the LORD give you everything your heart desires and always be your guide in life.

We will shout for joy every time Netzach blesses you by rallying around your banner in the name of the LORD; may Netzach fulfill all your desires through victory.

Other nations see their god in chariots and others in horses, but for us, we remember our LORD by His holy name.

When other nations fell, not to rise again, we have fallen, but the LORD raises us, and we will stay risen.

May the LORD grant salvation to his people. The King God will answer us on the days which we call upon Him.

Michael Harvey Koplitz

APPENDIX

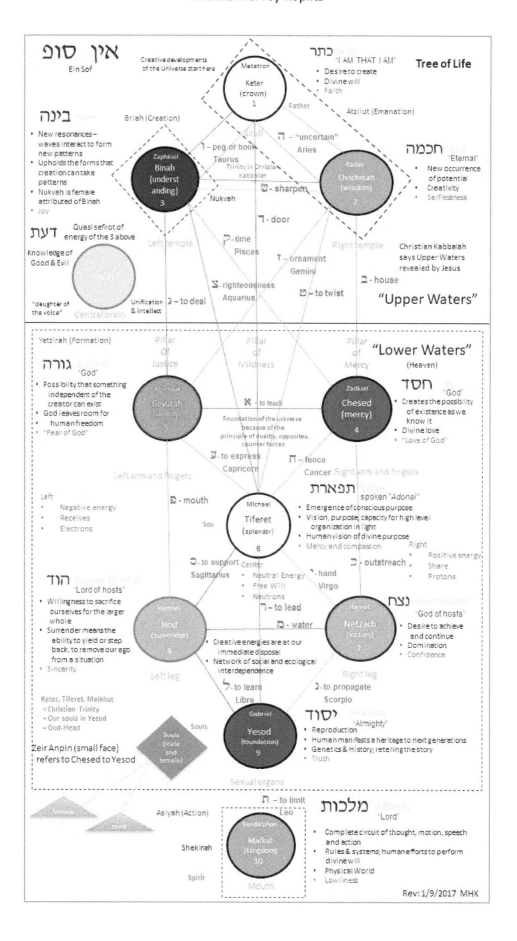

Tree of Life

אין סוף
Ein Sof

כתר
"I AM THAT I AM"
- Desire to create
- Divine will
- Faith

Creative developments of the Universe start here

Metatron
Keter (crown) 1

Father

Briah (Creation)

Atzilut (Emanation)

בינה
- New resonances – waves interact to form new patterns
- Upholds the forms that creation can take patterns
- Nukvah is female attributed of Binah
- Joy

ו – peg or hook
Taurus

Skull
Trinity in Christian Kabbalah

ה – "uncertain"
Aries

חכמה
"Eternal"
- New occurrence of potential
- Creativity
- Selflessness

Zaphkiel
Binah (understanding) 3

ש - sharpen

Nukvah

Raziel
Chochmah (wisdom) 2

דעת
Knowledge of Good & Evil

Quasi sefirot of energy of the 3 above

ד - door

Daat

ק - time
Pisces

ז - ornament
Gemini

Christian Kabbalah says Upper Waters revealed by Jesus

"daughter of the voice"

Central brain

Left temple

Right temple

Unification & intellect

ג – to deal

צ - righteousness
Aquarius

ב - house

"Upper Waters"

ט - to twist

Yetzirah (Formation)

Pillar Of Justice

Pillar of Mildness

Pillar of Mercy

"Lower Waters"
(Heaven)

גורה
"God"
- Possibility that something independent of the creator can exist
- God leaves room for human freedom
- "Fear of God"

Khamael
Gevurah (severity) 5

א – to teach

Foundation of the universe because of the principle of duality, opposites, counter forces

חסד
"God"
- Creates the possibility of existence as we know it
- Divine love
- "Love of God"

Zadkiel
Chesed (mercy) 4

ע - to express
Capricorn

ח – fence
Cancer

Right arm and fingers

Left arm and fingers

Left
- Negative energy
- Receives
- Electrons

תפארת
spoken "Adonai"
- Emergence of conscious purpose
- Vision, purpose, capacity for high level organization in light
- Human vision of divine purpose
- Mercy and compassion

פ - mouth

Michael
Tiferet (splendor) 6

Son

Right
- Positive energy
- Share
- Protons

כ - outreach

הוד
"Lord of hosts"
- Willingness to sacrifice ourselves for the larger whole
- Surrender means the ability to yield or step back, to remove our ego from a situation
- Sincerity

Center
- Neutral Energy
- Free Will
- Neutrons

י - hand
Virgo

ס - to support
Sagittarius

ר - to lead

מ - water

נצח
"God of hosts"
- Desire to achieve and continue
- Domination
- Confidence

Raphael
Hod (surrender) 8

Haniel
Netzach (victory) 7

Left leg

Creative energies are at our immediate disposal
Network of social and ecological interdependence

Right leg

Keter, Tiferet, Malkhut
= Christian Trinity
+ Our souls in Yesod
= God-Head

ל - to learn
Libre

נ - to propagate
Scorpio

Zeir Anpin (small face) refers to Chesed to Yesod

Souls

Souls (male and female)

Gabriel
Yesod (foundation) 9

יסוד
"Almighty"
- Reproduction
- Human manifests a heritage to next generations
- Genetics & History; retelling the story
- Truth

Sexual organs

female

male

ת – to limit
Leo

מלכות
"Lord"

Asiyah (Action)

Shekinah

Sandalphon
Malkut (kingdom) 10

- Complete circuit of thought, motion, speech and action
- Rules & systems; human efforts to perform divine will
- Physical World
- Lowliness

Spirit

Mouth

Rev: 1/9/2017 MHK

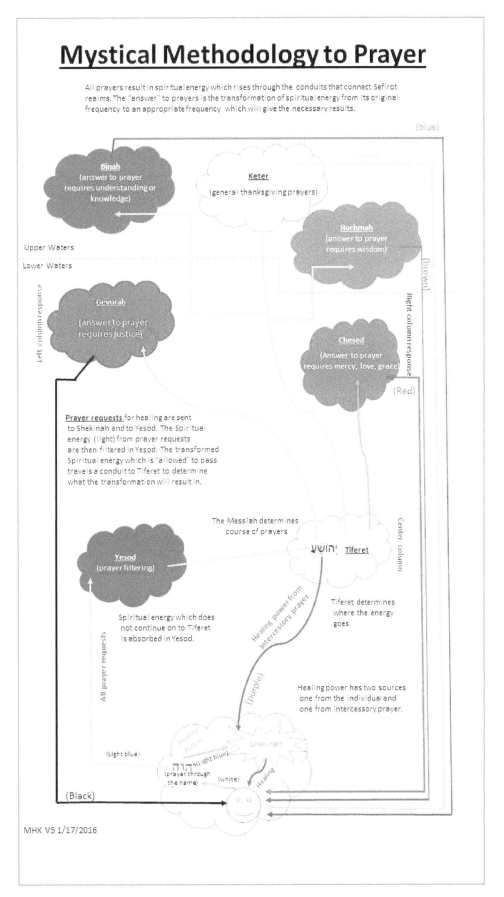

Mystical Methodology to Prayer

All prayers result in spiritual energy which rises through the conduits that connect Sefirot realms. The "answer" to prayers is the transformation of spiritual energy from its original frequency to an appropriate frequency which will give the necessary results.

(blue)

Binah
(answer to prayer requires understanding or knowledge)

Keter
(general thanksgiving prayers)

Hochmah
(answer to prayer requires wisdom)

Upper Waters

Lower Waters

Left column response

Gevurah
(answer to prayer requires justice)

(brown)

Right column response

Chesed
(Answer to prayer requires mercy, love, grace)

(Red)

Prayer requests for healing are sent to Shekinah and to Yesod. The Spiritual energy (light) from prayer requests are then filtered in Yesod. The transformed Spiritual energy which is "allowed" to pass travels a conduit to Tiferet to determine what the transformation will result in.

The Messiah determines course of prayers

יהושע   **Tiferet**

Center column

Yesod
(prayer filtering)

Spiritual energy which does not continue on to Tiferet is absorbed in Yesod.

Tiferet determines where the energy goes.

Healing power from intercessory prayer

(Purple)

Healing power has two sources one from the individual and one from intercessory prayer.

All prayer requests

Healing prayer

(light blue)

Shekinah

יהוה
(prayer through the name)

(white)

Healing

(Light blue)

(Black)

MHK V5 1/17/2016

Chambers of Aba and Ima of Briyah

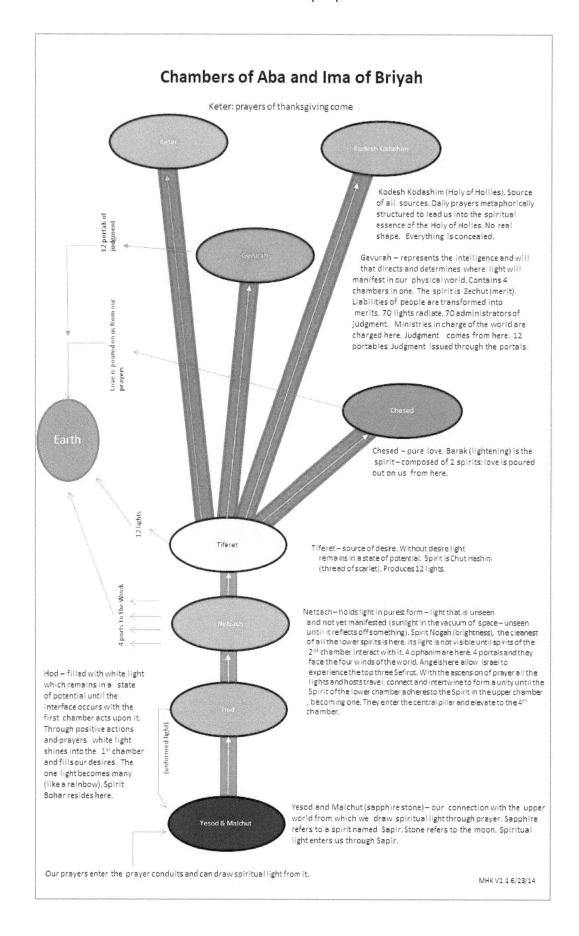

Keter: prayers of thanksgiving come

Keter

Kodesh Kodashim

Kodesh Kodashim (Holy of Hollies). Source of all sources. Daily prayers metaphorically structured to lead us into the spiritual essence of the Holy of Holies. No real shape. Everything is concealed.

12 portals of judgment

Gevurah

Gevurah – represents the intelligence and will that directs and determines where light will manifest in our physical world. Contains 4 chambers in one. The spirit is Zechut (merit). Liabilities of people are transformed into merits. 70 lights radiate. 70 administrators of judgment. Ministries in charge of the world are charged here. Judgment comes from here. 12 portables. Judgment issued through the portals.

Love is poured on us from our prayers

Chesed

Earth

Chesed – pure love. Barak (lightening) is the spirit – composed of 2 spirits: love is poured out on us from here.

12 lights

Tiferet

Tiferet – source of desire. Without desire light remains in a state of potential. Spirit is Chut Hashini (thread of scarlet). Produces 12 lights.

4 ports to the Winds

Netzach

Netzach – holds light in purest form – light that is unseen and not yet manifested (sunlight in the vacuum of space – unseen until it reflects off something). Spirit Nogah (brightness), the cleanest of all the lower spirits is here. Its light is not visible until spirits of the 2nd chamber interact with it. 4 ophanim are here. 4 portals and they face the four winds of the world. Angels here allow Israel to experience the top three Sefirot. With the ascension of prayer all the lights and hosts travel, connect and intertwine to form a unity until the Spirit of the lower chamber adheres to the Spirit in the upper chamber, becoming one. They enter the central pillar and elevate to the 4th chamber.

Hod – filled with white light which remains in a state of potential until the interface occurs with the first chamber acts upon it. Through positive actions and prayers white light shines into the 1st chamber and fills our desires. The one light becomes many (like a rainbow). Spirit Bohar resides here.

(unformed light)

Hod

Yesod & Malchut

Yesod and Malchut (sapphire stone) – our connection with the upper world from which we draw spiritual light through prayer. Sapphire refers to a spirit named Sapir. Stone refers to the moon. Spiritual light enters us through Sapir.

Our prayers enter the prayer conduits and can draw spiritual light from it.

MHK V1.1 6/23/14

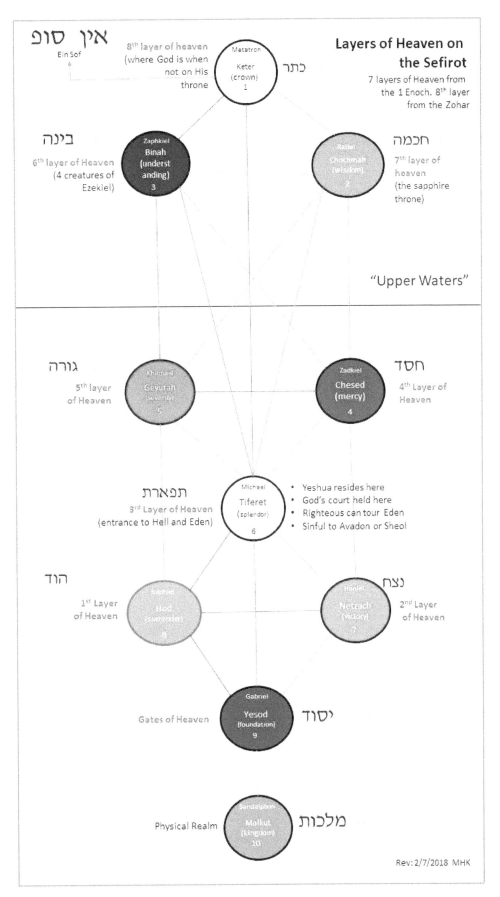